TRANSFORMATION THROUGH ACTIONS

Your personal growth roadmap:
Unlock your immense & yet underutilized potential!

ABHISHEK BUDHRAJA

INDIA · SINGAPORE · MALAYSIA

Copyright © Abhishek Budhraja 2023
All Rights Reserved.

ISBN 979-8-89133-639-1

This book has been published with all efforts taken to make the material error-free after the consent of the author. However, the author and the publisher do not assume and hereby disclaim any liability to any party for any loss, damage, or disruption caused by errors or omissions, whether such errors or omissions result from negligence, accident, or any other cause.

While every effort has been made to avoid any mistake or omission, this publication is being sold on the condition and understanding that neither the author nor the publishers or printers would be liable in any manner to any person by reason of any mistake or omission in this publication or for any action taken or omitted to be taken or advice rendered or accepted on the basis of this work. For any defect in printing or binding the publishers will be liable only to replace the defective copy by another copy of this work then available.

CONTENTS

PROLOGUE

Back in the early days of my career, I worked with GE. We used to have a term there: NIH, which stands for "Not Invented Here."

It was not used to dismiss things that weren't designed internally. Instead, it emphasized how we'd take existing concepts and effectively improvise and adapt them in our context. The best example of using a concept like Lean Six Sigma, which was basically from manufacturing, improvising, and adapting it in the service sector.

In the spirit of this approach, let me share the ACTIONS framework. While the main framework and the concept are my brainchild, arising from my own thoughts and experiences, it's crucial to mention that I've incorporated the brilliance of many remarkable individuals into this framework, pieces that resonate with the overall theme. I have shared their names as well.

Just like we embraced the "Not Invented Here" concept at GE, here too, I've drawn upon the wisdom and experiences of others to enhance the framework's effectiveness. It's a testament to the collaborative power of ideas and the beautiful synergy of shared inspiration.

As you dive into this book, you will see that I have shared numerous personal experiences that resonate with the framework. Although I may not have initially recognized the lessons within those experiences, I later discovered their value while on a journey of self-discovery.

Through this book, I intend to guide you through the ACTIONS framework for designing your life as it's meant to be. I hope that what I am about to share helps you choose between three options:

"Present self," "Reinvented self," and "Dreamer self." Don't feel pressured to make a choice just yet; I'll provide more clarity on this matter later.

Before reading, I want to make it clear that this is all about empowering you to take action and design a blueprint of life you truly desire. This will ultimately inspire and guide you toward the necessary steps to turn your aspirations into reality.

INTRODUCTION

"Manzil Milegi Bhatak Kar Hi Sahi, Gumrah To Woh Hai Jo Ghar Se Nikle hi Nahi."

– Mirza Ghalib

"The destination will be reached only by wandering, the one who never leaves his home is misguided." English translation of the above quote by Mirza Ghalib

Imagine waking up one fine morning, ten years from now, and realizing that your life doesn't truly reflect who you are and what you're capable of. You have ample possessions, yet you go through your days feeling stuck and stagnant, simply wasting your potential.

Perhaps you've always had a talent for connecting with people, or maybe you've caught yourself thinking about pursuing a hobby, a business idea, or an excursion, but you've settled for a job that drains you. The truth is that you have it in you; you possess everything needed to transform from 'what is' to 'what could be.'

What if you could tap into the untapped potential within you to live a life of purpose, passion, and profound fulfillment? Are you ready to design the finest version of yourself?

Before going any further with this book, let me clarify one thing. This book is not merely a collection of more information. I'm sure you've already accumulated a lot of it over the years. My intent for you is to provide you with a framework that will help you explore and unleash the potential that either you didn't know existed within you or didn't really try to harness. It has remained underutilized, all this while waiting to be set free. This is about transformation, and more specifically, your transformation from your true current "As Is" reality to a desired aspirational "To Be." This journey is about self-discovery, self-belief, and self-empowerment.

How will that be possible? Well, through ACTIONS!

I am sure your journey through life so far has been great, marked by success and happiness. How about designing one NOW, if it hasn't been meaningful and fulfilling?

Let me tell you a secret: you already possess the key ingredients within you. All you need is a little bit of:

- Time – Not just to read the book and be done with it, but to act as well.
- Commitment – To consistently keep moving forward despite obstacles.
- Framework - Methodology to organize your thoughts and guide your efforts effectively.
- And, of course, lots of actions.

Why? Because it's YOUR transformational journey.

By the end of this journey, you'll stand tall, gazing at the mirror with a newfound appreciation for the incredible person staring back at you. You'll understand that the potential within you is as vast as the universe itself, and you are capable of achieving greatness beyond your wildest imagination.

Let's face it; you've spent years working hard and helping others achieve their goals, such as parents, society, customers, bosses, management, organizations. And like many others, you have been convincing yourself that this is the best option. Is it?

It's important that you are assisting others in reaching their goals, but at the same time, you need to nurture your ambitions, pursue your dreams, and aspirations. Remember, personal growth and development are also important, and your efforts should be aligned with realizing your aspirational life.

"Exploration is the key to discovery. And without exploration, there will be no discovery."

There are immense possibilities out there and opportunities to turn those possibilities into reality. Possibilities that once seemed attainable, but we deviated from that path, treading the most obvious one or choosing whatever came our way. As a result, we now feel stuck and unwilling to change.

How about transforming your life right now? And I'm not suggesting a completely new path; you might find a new one or redesign the existing one, aligning it with your purpose. As I mentioned earlier, the possibilities are immense.

Trust me, the journey of self-exploration leading to transformation will be the best journey you've embarked on so far, on your path to becoming the finest version of yourself.

The world is brimming with possibilities and opportunities. There are options, and more will become available as you explore. Begin your exploration to build your well-designed life.

Of course, this journey is not for everyone, especially those who live by excuses like "there's no time to do anything else" or "it's too late now," and so on. That's perfectly fine – you're the captain of your life boat. But if you find yourself:

- Lacking energy and excitement in what you are doing.
- Feeling disengaged and dispassionate about work and people.
- Lacking inspiration to go beyond your assigned tasks.
- Not feeling like contributing more than what is required.
- Constantly questioning your purpose, asking why you are doing what you are doing.
- Not finding things challenging or not feeling like taking on new challenges.
- Experiencing flattened learning.
- Having no clarity on your goals.
- Feeling like everything is a drag.
- Experiencing life as a routine.

If you are experiencing most or all of the symptoms mentioned above, and they are causing you stress or anxiety, you are clearly trapped in your life. If you are willing to transform that, then you must take action now.

And when you start your journey of transformation, be prepared to be amazed. I guarantee that you will be.

Contract:

Before you embark on this journey of transformation, I want you to commit wholeheartedly to the path ahead. Remember, commitment is the cornerstone of any meaningful change. To guide you through this transformative adventure, we'll be using the ACTIONS framework, which comprises six key milestones, each with specific actions and timelines. Are you ready to commit to this journey of growth and self-discovery? Let's dive in!

Commit to the Journey - Write down your reasons for committing to this journey of personal growth. What are you hoping to achieve by the end of this journey?

Set Timelines - Assign a realistic timeline to each milestone. How much time do you think you'll need to complete the actions associated with each milestone? Be honest with yourself about the time you can dedicate to this journey.

Declare Your Commitment - Write a commitment statement that summarizes your dedication to completing the milestones and actions within the specified timelines. Sign it as a personal contract to yourself.

Track Your Progress - Establish a journal or digital tracker to record your progress. Consistently update your tracker with completed actions, achieved milestones, and any insights you've gained.

Celebrate Milestones - As you accomplish each milestone, take a moment to celebrate your progress. Reward yourself with something meaningful to commemorate your achievements.

Reflect and Adjust - At regular intervals, review your commitment statement, milestones, and progress. Reflect on what's working well and consider any necessary adjustments. Be flexible and compassionate with yourself.

Let's get Designing

The purpose of this book is to provide you with the tools necessary for your journey of self-discovery. As you embark on this path, you will gain clarity, explore possibilities, and construct a life that both excites and fulfills you. This transformation is achievable through your commitment to taking actions and designing a fulfilling life – it is transformation through ACTIONS.

Throughout this journey, you will shift your life from its current reality, the "As Is," to your desired reality, the "To Be." You will discover who you truly are rather than conforming to who you should be.

This book is grounded in the ACTIONS framework that I developed during my own journey of self-transformation. I won't claim to be completely transformed, as it's an ongoing process, but I know I'm on the right path.

By following this framework, you will define your life's overarching objective and systematically break it down into manageable, short-term goals. You'll make progress step by step, celebrating each success and cultivating a habit of success.

Instead of fixating solely on end goals and adhering to a predetermined course, I propose a different approach. Define your aspirations and key milestones, shift your focus from the ultimate outcome to what comes next. Explore opportunities while striving to achieve these milestones, adapt and improve your strategy, and continuously learn and progress. This dynamic process will either lead you to your defined goal or something even better. The key is to learn, adapt, and consistently act along the way.

Imagine taking your car out to reach a destination. Do you keep thinking only about the destination, or do you navigate each twist and turn, maneuvering through challenges and making real-time decisions? You move forward towards your destination, exploring better routes/options, improvising, and learning as you encounter challenges while driving—traffic jams, accidents, and many more—overcoming each as they come.

As they say, the "Journey is as important as the destination."

Relevant goals:

At times, we find ourselves relentlessly pursuing goals, and upon achieving them, we experience a momentary sense of happiness. However, we still feel unsatisfied. Often, this dissatisfaction arises because the accomplished goal lacks alignment with our true aspirations, our life's purpose.

Many times, I hear from friends, colleagues, and clients who are fixated on the pursuit of accumulating wealth. People may not explicitly state it, but their actions unmistakably convey that desire. Further inquiry often reveals the following reasons:
1. Lack of clarity.
2. Pursuit of possessions to elevate social standing.
3. To compete with others.

All of these result in a continuous chase of one thing after another, eventually reaching a point where you have many things but nothing relevant or of little relevance to your life's true essence.

"You can't be what you want to be but you can be what you are" - *Jay Shetty*

Every life harbors aspirations and a purpose, yet most lack clarity about it. Consequently, we spend a lifetime following and competing with each other, accumulating material possessions that are often unrelated to that purpose.

Achieving your goals depends on the actions you take to get there. However, true transformation goes beyond a mere series of steps aimed at reaching a desired objective. It involves embracing the journey marked by exploration, learning, and celebrating personal growth and self-improvement, all towards becoming your best self. Most importantly, it entails recognizing that your genuine potential is considerably greater than you believe.

Enjoy the journey, and always remember that success is not solely defined by what you possess but by the path you intentionally design to fulfill your aspirations. This path is not always convenient or obvious but is deliberately crafted by you.

Transformational change demands focused efforts, consistent actions, and a great deal of patience. There is a wealth of untapped potential within each of us, and when harnessed correctly, it opens up a multitude of possibilities that positively impact all dimensions of our lives.

CHAOS

We often find ourselves in a constant state of chaos, either by pretending to be someone we are not or by engaging in activities that do not align with our true selves. This ongoing chaos leads us to spend most of our time trying to figure out what comes next or putting out fires to resolve issues within ourselves and others. This consumes a significant amount of our energy and time, ultimately leaving us feeling stuck and foregoing the exploration of possibilities, settling for the status quo.

Explore to discover your path: Personally, I have made numerous discoveries about myself through exploration, and I continue to do so. In this process of exploration, I have astonished myself by doing things that defy my pre-existing beliefs—things I could never have imagined doing before.

Throughout this journey, I encourage you to amaze yourself. Who knows where your exploration will lead you on your life's path? When you begin experiencing those magical moments of breaking your own defined barriers, I'm certain you'll desire more.

How to make the most out of this experience?

Have faith in the process, be open and honest with yourself, put in focused efforts, and exercise patience. It's a transformation journey, and you will encounter various obstacles. Interestingly, most of these obstacles originate from within you, anchored in your mind.

For many years, I had contemplated quitting my job and pursuing my passions. However, I was stuck in a routine that was merely about making ends meet, leaving me feeling stagnant and irrelevant. I was frustrated with what I was doing, yet I couldn't take action because of those beliefs that were deeply rooted in my mind.

"Excellence is in our beliefs and focused actions." We all have the potential to be magnificent.

ACTIONS framework works

A quick Google search will reveal numerous books, courses, and training programs promising transformative change. "There is no right or wrong option unless you have tried them."

Transformation is not a quick fix, and I'm not attempting to diminish the credibility of those books, courses, or training programs. After all, I also gained valuable knowledge to transform my reality. There is no one-size-fits-all formula. What's often missing is the motivation to explore and take action. Each individual is unique, and it's that uniqueness within you that you need to explore. The ACTIONS framework is my gift to you in your journey of self-discovery and designing a life that's meant to be. Through this framework, I have endeavored to outline a logical and simplified process.

I want you to explore yourself and find answers by following this straightforward process. All it takes is your commitment and some actions to design your life or career. And if you design it well, happiness and success will follow. But you need to:
1. Be honest, not for others, but for your own growth.
2. If you're unsure, trust your initial instincts. Often, they hold the truth.
3. Avoid overanalyzing or overthinking. This is a habit for most of us, one that hasn't served us well in the past. If it hasn't served us in the past, why would it serve us now? Overthinking hinders productive action because it traps you in a mental loop of "What if" and other unproductive thoughts, resulting in inaction and wasting time and energy.

4. Commit to the journey and maintain consistency in your actions.

"Price of greatness is responsibility" Winston Churchill

Achieving what we strive for requires unwavering commitment. Our transformation won't happen overnight, and we'll need to take some easy, some hard, and some unconventional actions. In the past, when faced with difficult situations, we might have stopped ourselves, resorting to what we always do, which is retreating to our comfort zone.

This pattern needs to change. Transforming dreams into reality necessitates taking positive actions, and while it may seem simple, it's not easy. It begins with making a promise to ourselves that we will change and keeping that promise. We must do this for ourselves, not for others. Initially, people around us may feel uncomfortable, find it strange, or be surprised. Some may even try to discourage us (similar to smoking buddies trying to get you back to smoking), but eventually, we will find support from them if we remain steadfast in our commitment. Even if they don't support us, remember that this journey is yours, not theirs.

"Without commitment you will never start and without consistency you will never finish" Denzel Washington

5. Have a right mindset (will talk more about this later)

So, here I am, offering this book as a testament to one of the numerous awe-inspiring moments I've encountered on my journey. Honestly, as part of my personal transformation, I have experienced and done things that I couldn't even have imagined a few years back when I was experiencing all those symptoms of feeling stagnant while sitting in a cubicle.

Are you ready for self-discovery and your transformation?
First, let's start with a simple question:

- What do you do?
- How many years have you been doing what you are doing (study/job/business, etc.)?

- Do you feel what you are doing is meaningful, fulfilling, and brings you happiness?
- That was pretty simple, right?

Now that we know what you do and how long you've been doing it, let's dive into a different kind of question.

Imagine you're planning a road trip, and you're curious about the weather conditions. What would be the ideal temperature for your adventure? You check the weather app and find that the air pressure is 1015 hPa, the temperature is 30°C, and the relative humidity is 30%. What do you think the weather might be like?

No worries, you're not alone. Just like others, you'd turn to your trusty navigation app for directions on your road trip, there are resources like Google to help you understand the atmospheric conditions and their effects on your journey.

Here's a thought-provoking one:
Why are you doing what you are doing? Or what's the purpose of your life, and are your actions aligned with that purpose?
Take a couple of minutes to describe the purpose of your life.

1...2...3, Time's up! So, have you been able to articulate your purpose clearly? If you haven't, imagine going on a road trip with a goal in mind but no GPS, maps, or idea of the direction where you should be heading. That's how it feels.

If you have articulated your purpose, is your current path aligned with your dreams? rate yourself on a scale of 1 to 10.

Explain why you have given yourself this rating.

In this digital age, you may get answers to many questions by doing a simple Google search, but there is no Google for your life questions. I wish there were one; things would have been so simple.

98% of all of us will die without fulfilling our dreams, and 92% of the people who define their goals never actually achieve them.

Where do you currently stand in these statistics? Do you belong to the 98% or the elite 2%?

It may seem absurd to ask if you believe you are part of the 98% and if you'd like to join the 2%. Naturally, no one would say 'no' to that. Well, you have the potential to be part of that 2%; you just haven't realized it yet.

The point I'd like to make here is that everyone wishes to have a fulfilling, exciting, meaningful, and balanced life. That is a separate fact; many of us have no idea what that life is like along with being unclear about our purpose in life.

And if you lack clarity, that's entirely normal because you're among the vast majority of people who have been living life on autopilot, following the path that has been laid out for them.

A few years ago, there was a study[1] conducted in the USA. According to the study, people with a purpose in life "live longer." About 7,000 people between the ages of 20 and 70 were studied over a span of 14 years. Many of us, over the years, have become accustomed to whatever life throws at us and have adjusted to it.

We were curious in the beginning when we were young kids. I'm sure you all remember the times when you would irritate your parents by asking the "why" question repeatedly about everything you came across. As the years passed by, we stopped asking those questions as life happened to most of us. We were pushed into a world where everybody was running to attain something. As school and college kids, we chased higher grades because that's what our teachers and parents wanted us to achieve. Often, our passions didn't align with their vision because they believed those interests wouldn't lead to wealth and success.

Parents, teachers, and society instilled in us the belief that higher grades would lead to the best jobs and a happier life. So, the notion that successful people are happier was ingrained in our minds, along with the idea that success is synonymous with money, a house, status, and so on.

---

[1] Study conducted by Carleton University in Canada and the University of Rochester Medical Center. Published in the journal Psychological Science in 2014

Expectations and responsibilities gradually took over, guiding us onto paths we might not have chosen if left to our own devices.

Ask yourself this question: Are you currently living the life you genuinely desired, the life you dreamt of, free from any external expectations? Ask yourself:

- Are you happy with what you are doing?
- Do you find your life meaningful, fulfilling, and balanced?
- Given a choice, would you stick to the same path or choose something different? (It's okay if you don't know it now; just follow your instincts.)

Many of you might say that you didn't have a choice, especially when it comes to academics. Studies show that three-quarters of college graduates end up in fields unrelated to their majors.

In my corporate experience, I have encountered many individuals who excelled in their roles, despite not having studied for them. Some were MBBS graduates, while others were engineers working in corporate jobs unrelated to their studies. I'm not suggesting that they are doing anything wrong; I'm simply making a point. Perhaps they figured it out a bit later.

The truth is, life happened for most of us. You graduated from college, got a job, and at first, you were excited because it was challenging and fulfilling. You might have thought that life was all set. The next steps usually involved getting married, having kids, retiring, and then embarking on a world trip to fulfill your dreams.

Let me ask you this: Do you still feel the same way now? If you do, you're probably still in the honeymoon phase, have given up, or perhaps you've figured things out.

However, if over the years, you've become accustomed to living a certain way and haven't paid much attention to the purpose of your life, you might be living your life on autopilot.

Everyone agrees that "the only constant in life is change," and it's true. Look around you; the world is in a perpetual state of transformation. Yet, changing oneself is one of the most formidable tasks. If our car keeps breaking down, we can either change or repair the car. But when it comes to altering our life, we often can't or won't because it seems too challenging, and we've grown comfortable with where we are. We fear rocking the boat.

We can't because of the obstacles, and we don't because we believe these obstacles are too tough to overcome. The reality is that most of these hurdles exist in our minds, stemming from beliefs and habits that don't serve us well. In 99% of cases, we fail to take action because we lack clarity, experience self-doubt, fear, or lack confidence.

I was never a very social person, and the idea of publishing an article or a blog and sharing it on social media was something I could never fathom. I was afraid of rejection and didn't believe I could write. But I did it—not just once, but multiple times in succession. In all honesty, my motivation wasn't solely driven by a love for writing; it was also fueled by a desire to break through my mental barriers. Now, here I am, writing this book.

The truth is that we all have enormous potential, but due to our lack of clarity and our self-limiting beliefs, we often feel stuck. The only clear alternative that comes to mind is to go with the flow, akin to getting up in the morning, getting into your car, and driving somewhere with no destination in mind. You just keep driving, and when you come to an intersection, you either turn around or start reciting "eenie meenie miney mo."

Do abilities differ person to person?

Indeed, there are certain innate traits that influence our abilities, but that doesn't imply our abilities are fixed or stagnant. They can be developed over time through deliberate effort and a growth-oriented mindset.

We all possess the potential for growth and improvement within our reach, and success isn't reserved for a select few. Some people achieve great heights, while others remain in the shadows of uncertainty.

You've likely encountered remarkable individuals who've realized their dreams. Their secret isn't some elusive gift; it's having clarity and an unwavering belief in their abilities!

These successful individuals aren't immune to worries or doubts, but they maintain confidence and never lose sight of their goals. They innovate, adapt, and confront challenges with conviction, commitment, and accountability for their actions. They believe in their capacity to overcome obstacles.

So, if you don't know where you're going, everything else becomes secondary. What's the point of a journey if it doesn't lead where it should?

Let me ask you those questions once more: Why are you doing what you are doing? What is the purpose of your life, and is what you are doing aligned with that purpose?

I urge you to be honest with yourself when answering these questions. You don't need to answer them because I've asked you to; you need to believe in these questions and answer them truthfully to embark on your transformation journey.

Every transformation begins with awareness and acceptance of the need to do so. Don't become fixated on the idea that your current situation is the best you can have. Instead, explore and take actions to turn your dream reality into a success.

Success isn't solely about achieving the end goal or the desired reality of "To Be." While that is undoubtedly important, it's also about progressing at every step along the way as you gain clarity, face challenges, and design and realize the life you've dreamed of.

Success isn't solely about what you possess; it's about the satisfaction you derive from the progress you make while overcoming obstacles and challenges to attain your desires.

Let me share this with you: once you've tasted success, no matter how small, it becomes addictive; you'll crave more of it. You don't become a Rockstar overnight; you start by crawling before you can walk! Small successes build confidence, and before you know it, you'll navigate obstacles like a pro. Transforming yourself requires focus, effort, and a great deal of patience.

What you need is to cultivate the habit of success, and that will happen gradually, one step at a time. You may encounter failures along the way, but it's better to stumble and then rise, taking small steps toward a larger goal, rather than aiming for something big and risking complete failure. The key is to start with simplicity and find success in those small steps. This not only makes you feel good but also builds the confidence to progress toward your larger goals. Remember, it's one step at a time.

Think of this journey as designing your dream life, one step at a time. Each tiny success brings you closer to the grand prize, and trust me, the journey itself is an integral part of the adventure!

The truth is, if your dreams and goals were easy to achieve, you wouldn't derive as much enjoyment from accomplishing them. It's not just the goals themselves that are challenging; the journey to reach them is equally challenging, and that's what makes the process enjoyable and exciting when you eventually achieve them.

BREAKING PERSONAL BOUNDARIES: CONFORMANCE TO TRANSFORMATION

"The difference between falling short or fulfilling your true potential is how well you've designed your life."

I spent nearly 20 years in the corporate world, working for various multinational companies. Initially, it was all quite exciting, but over time, that excitement began to wane. I liked my job and was proficient at it, but as the years passed, I couldn't shake the restlessness within me – a sense that life held more than what I was experiencing.

Have you ever felt like this?

- Lacking passion for what you do, simply going through the motions of your daily routine.
- Feeling comfortable with your situation, even if it lacks meaning and fulfillment.
- Unwilling to challenge the status quo and push yourself beyond the boundaries you've set based on your perceived capabilities.

As a result, you may find yourself falling short of your true potential, engaging in activities that are meaningless and serve no real purpose. There's a clear distinction between being good or mediocre at something and truly excelling at it.

It's easy to become trapped within the boundaries we set for ourselves, never daring to step outside and explore the limitless potential that exists beyond those boundaries.

I made a conscious decision not to be just another cog in the corporate wheel.

There's a significant difference between liking something and truly loving it. While our jobs may offer security, comfort, and luxuries, many of us yearn for something more, something that ignites our passion every single day.

Playing it safe, being a conformist

As a successful corporate professional earning a seven-figure salary, it might sound great, but in reality, I had lost my passion for what I was doing, leading to anxiety and frustration.

It was more like operating on autopilot from 9 to 5 every day, literally dragging myself to the workplace, bringing no value to the job or myself, doing nothing more than a job, doing the same things day after day, without knowing why I was doing what I was doing. It offered no challenges anymore.

To add to it, clarity of what's next and life's goal was missing, and without it, taking action to change their circumstances seemed impossible. I could have looked for another job, but deep down I knew that would have meant moving from one rut to another. I had ideas to do things differently but lacked the initiative to take action.

I was in my comfort zone, following the common path as most of us do, finding happiness in material possessions, assuming what I have is the best option available there is. Conventional wisdom says happiness is determined by one's income and material possessions, among other things. Isn't this how we have been groomed by society, schools, parents?

I struggled to wipe the slate clean, start afresh, and create a life that is meaningful and fulfilling.

I was hoping to get fired

You heard that right. If I continued this path, it seemed likely that I would experience a breakdown or some sort of medical issue. There was hardly any excitement towards the job, and on many occasions, even contemplated resigning. That seemed like a good idea but couldn't muster the courage to take that step. Multiple contributors like fear of losing that comfortable seven-figure salary, fearing the unknown, lacking clarity, stopped me from taking that step. Sounds familiar!

This might sound crazy to a lot of people since I was not able to take action, so I was hoping for some divine intervention. Frankly, I even entertained thoughts, at times, of experiencing a change in my employment situation. And guess what? I realized the law of attraction does work.

On this particular day, I was expecting an increment after receiving an excellent annual rating. Something unexpected happened when my manager and the HR head asked to meet me in a conference room. This was a bit surprising because the manager usually shares good news. Despite the overall organization situation, I said to myself that maybe this year they were being exceptionally generous with the salary hike. However, the meeting took a different turn. Due to recent changes and downsizing, my role had become redundant, and consequently, they had to let me go. They offered a golden handshake along with a reasonable severance pay-out.

Normally, this would be a source of sadness, stress, and anxiety for people like me. But for some strange reason, I wasn't feeling that. It was a bit of a shock, going through this ordeal as I wasn't expecting it. But honestly, I was not as sad as one might expect. At that moment, I would be wrong to say that I saw this as an opportunity to explore new possibilities. But I guess at a subconscious level, I was feeling relieved, and it seemed like I was free to explore. After all, change does open new possibilities. It's up to you how you deal with it.

So, here I was without a job, and it took me some time to realize that I had no plan either.

Having no job seemed worse than having a job, no matter how much you hate it, especially when one is not clear about the next steps. Also, because people around you don't expect to see you like that. I knew I needed to do something because I still had bills to pay and things to take care of, luckily no financial liabilities.

So, there I was, left with two options: look for a new job or the alternate option was to do what I really wanted to do, and honestly, at that particular moment, I had no idea. I did get some offers through friends and old colleagues, which I respectfully declined. Thanks to them, but this was not the path I wished to continue, at least not then. I probably would get stuck in yet another rut and be back where I started, so I didn't take that, and till date no regrets at all.

The challenge, considering an alternative path, was that I had to overcome my own self and confront my deeply ingrained impediments. These included habits that I had nurtured for ages, such as playing safe, avoiding risk, procrastinating, and, above that, gaining clarity.

Long back in 2016, I wanted to start a project in healthcare for which I did really good research. I created a project report, did some budgeting, etc., but kept delaying taking action, like seeking a funder and more. In my heart, I knew that it's a relevant idea because there is a need for it, but at most, I spoke with a few people, did a survey, and bought a domain; that's it.

Years of playing safe, avoiding risks, procrastinating. I was afraid as it was beyond my comfort zone. It meant breaking multiple beliefs such as "I am not sure if I will be able to do it," "I need to have all the answers before I approach someone," "can't make mistakes," and most importantly, "people from service backgrounds should continue in jobs rather than becoming entrepreneurs; that's a recipe for failure." This is one belief that even if you want to get over, you won't because people around you will keep reminding.

So, it is not a matter of just changing something, but what I need is Transformational change to a newer and empowered version of "Me." A big transformation from the old introverted self to the new, empowered version that I wanted to become. This meant unlearning many things and learning new things and motivating self every day to not give up.

It was a daunting journey, and I was not sure how long I would be able to keep going.

And then there was the potential for financial struggle too, not immediately, but at some point in the future as there was no incoming cash flow. I was running on my savings. Above that, I had to show people that I was busy and doing well because I wouldn't ask for any favors from friends and colleagues. I was trying to show a brave face to everyone, and within, I was shit scared, battling inner fears and uncertainty.

From optimizing processes to optimizing people to be their best selves

I have always been an ideator (some may call it a daydreamer), thinking of new ways to create or do things. Lots of ideas and low on action.

My current situation did provide an opportunity for me to give shape to those ideas, a possibility. So, I began my journey, started afresh at 44. It was like the slate wiped clean waiting to be filled. Opportunity to fill it with whatever I want.

I learned, tried, and created things, constantly pushing the boundaries of my perceived capabilities. It wasn't an easy path – had to figure things out on my own without much support.

With time and experience, realizing that we can do more than what we think we can, I wanted to help people like myself who are stuck, overwhelmed, and confused about what their next step should be. I needed to figure out how I can. I was a coach and quality professional driving operational/process excellence. I realized that we all make plans to change or transform, but what's lacking was actions, so that was it. The spark ignited, me being a whiteboard person, I went straight to a whiteboard and started jotting stuff. There it was, I had the ACTIONS framework.

With my vast experience in operations and process excellence using continuous improvement methodologies, design thinking, problem-solving, coaching, and mentoring people, I developed a framework to take actions that help individuals be the best version of themselves.

In a real sense, it was a transition from optimizing business operations and processes to optimizing people, and it was a significant one. Processes and people are the foundation for performance excellence, driving personal and operational excellence. Processes are designed and driven by people. Imagine running an organization with employees who are not enthusiastic about their work. Imagine, huh! Just look around.

While doing so, I've done things I couldn't even imagine doing a couple of years ago. I've had so many "amaze me" moments. I realized I was holding myself back because of my limited view of my capability and, much more so, because of external influence. A few of the "amaze me" moments of stepping out of my comfort zone:

- I began training for a prestigious global organization. The stakes are pretty high when you are an external consultant providing training to different industry segments than as an employee. Despite the initial challenges, I have successfully carried out training sessions and continue to contribute significantly to the company's training initiatives.
- Pushing my boundaries, I adopted diverse training styles, fostering experiential learning beyond the ordinary. As an introvert, this personal transformation was remarkable. The feedback I received, including praise for my exceptional interpersonal skills and kinesthetic training approach, was incredibly rewarding.
- I developed ACTIONS, a powerful tool to help individuals discover and design their passions, aligning with their life's purpose. I started coaching, guiding individuals to unlock their full potential using this framework.
- I founded Immensa Consulting, where I single-handedly managed every aspect, from planning and registration to logo design, marketing, website development, compliance, and taxes.

- I took up some challenging projects.
- I learned digital marketing, including funnel creation, landing page setup, video and audio editing, content writing, running ads, and started blogging and writing articles.
- And now, I've authored this very book.

And there's more. Some of it aligned with the goal of helping individuals be the best version of themselves, and some to quench my thirst for adventure (I'll share more about this later). All of them, however, have a common thread; they require me to constantly challenge my self-imposed limitations.

In all honesty, I accomplished more in three years than in the last five years in a corporate role. I don't intend to boast, but just to make a point that we all have the opportunity to be great, and yet we decide to settle for much less.

The best part of it all is that this transformation wasn't by chance; it was a deliberate design, a conscious choice. And I'm loving it.

True happiness is the by-product of doing what you love, pursuing your passion, and living a purposeful life

1. We limit ourselves by what we believe we are capable of doing, instead of exploring our strengths or what we are truly capable of doing. As a result, we are not living or fulfilling our true potential.
2. Fear, self-doubt, anxiety, overthinking, helplessness, and hesitations will pull us down. There will be a lot of bad days, and then there will be very few good days. The key is to keep motivating yourself every day and take small and doable actions to keep the momentum of progress going. Circumstances, situations, and people will pull you down, and it's easy to give up. The key is to keep progressing, instead of giving up or getting overwhelmed.
3. Happiness is not in having material things, having a great job, a role, etc. What good is it if after having all that you are still

looking for meaning and fulfillment in life or feeling stuck with your choices?

"Happiness is a by-product of what you do."

If you are passionate about what you are doing, working toward fulfilling your life's purpose, then happiness will have a much bigger meaning, and the satisfaction that you will derive will be immense. It's all about designing your life, and if you have designed it well, then money and all that material stuff that brings temporary happiness will still happen and maybe more.

Discover and design your passion to live your life's purpose

Each one of us has immense potential to do more than what we think we can, but that remains underutilized because we don't see beyond the boundaries that we have set for ourselves. Listen to what you say to yourself when faced with a challenge if you want to know your boundaries.

What we are doing might be a good option, but not necessarily the best, or it may be the best, but since you haven't designed it yourself with clarity of your aspirations, passion, purpose, and other factors, you're probably not aware of your full potential yet. We won't discover better options until we've explored them. Exploring new possibilities doesn't necessarily mean giving up on current pursuits. It's about designing options, either from scratch or by refining existing ones.

Quitting or giving up would be a big mistake that I realized later.

So, if you are in that state of chaos, stagnancy, there are three options:

1. Continue as you are, settling for what you have.
2. Wait for the appropriate opportunity to present itself. Most of the time, we will miss it because, one, we are champions of missed opportunities, and second, even if we want to, we will stop ourselves.

3. Take action NOW and design the life you truly desire.

    "Our life is the sum of all our choices" - Albert Camus

    "What 'we are' is the consequence of the choices we or others made for us in the past, and what we 'can be' is the consequence of the choice we make NOW!" You have the opportunity to be your best self, so design it now and design it well.

SUCCESS AND HAPPINESS

— Rollo May

Imagine a world where nine out of ten people conform to societal norms and expectations without questioning why they do what they do.

Our perception of happiness, in most cases, is not defined by us. Instead, it is instilled by external influences, including society, parents, teachers, and neighbors. We are taught that material possessions like money, status, and power bring us happiness, and so we relentlessly chase after them.

But the truth is, things like money, power, fame, etc., are indeed important and do bring temporary happiness. That's why we don't stop at one; we keep chasing the next one and then the next. The happiness you derive tends to fade after some time. They don't provide lasting fulfillment.

This is what we are taught right from the beginning, or at least during the time when I was in school and college. The unfortunate part is it still holds true. Get a good score so you can get into a good college and land a good job, buy luxuries for yourself to live a happy life, get married, and so on. You will be considered successful if you have money, status in society, a big house, and more, but the feeling within might be totally different.

It's a vicious spiral of trying to achieve more and better than what we currently have, which ends up leaving us unnecessarily and unreasonably busy, overwhelmed, and exhausted, doing things that are meaningless, unfulfilling, and adding no value to our lives.

If you don't believe this, then answer this: just remember the last major purchase you made. How long did the happiness last, or how long before you started running after the next level, which could be the next car, house, etc.?

Of course, there is no harm in that, but remember only a few succeed as per that definition, and yet many of them lead a meaningless, unfulfilled life, just running after things and more.

Stop running after happiness, as happiness is a by-product of doing what we are truly passionate about, aligned with our aspirations, serving our life's purpose, and constantly pushing boundaries to achieve it.

What if I told you that if you've designed your life right and are striving to make it a reality, happiness and success will follow?

Humans are, by design, explorers, but we stopped being one as we grew older and started being followers instead.

Are you living your aspirational life?

To break free from this pattern, it is essential to reflect on our own lives and assess the level of alignment between our aspirational life and our current reality. If there's a misalignment, we must ask ourselves if we are willing to continue living in a meaningless and unfulfilling reality, even if it comes with material gains.

Discover Your Aspirational Life

Objective: Help individuals reflect on their aspirational life, their passion, values, and goals. It helps them envision a life that aligns with their true self through self-exploration.

Instructions:
- Find a quiet, comfortable place where you won't be distracted for the next 10 minutes.
- Take a piece of paper and document your thoughts and responses.
- Be honest when you respond to the questions. Be honest not only to me but to yourself.

- Remember, the first thought that comes to your mind is often the most authentic one.
- Avoid over-analyzing or overthinking. We have been doing enough of that, and see where it has gotten us. Instead, embrace the process of exploration and discovery.
- Envision Your Aspirational Life: Ask yourself, "What is my aspirational life?"

Consider the life you envision for yourself, one that encompasses your passions and values. It may involve creative pursuits, meaningful relationships, personal growth, or making a positive impact on the world.

If you are amongst 90% of the population, then I am sure you don't even have that clarity and could spend hours, days figuring it out and yet be confused. But this is okay, as I didn't have it either, and you know. It's a journey, and it will keep evolving over the years.

As human beings, we are naturally inclined to explore and discover, and the more we explore, the more we discover and keep discovering. The act of exploring leads to new discoveries, which in turn fuels our desire to explore further. It is a virtuous cycle of expanding our knowledge, pushing boundaries, and embracing the unknown. Each new experience, encounter, or knowledge that we gain broadens our understanding and our perspective.

It's a continuous process; the more we get into it, the more we discover, learn, and grow.

- Now that you have maybe written your aspirations, answer the following questions keeping in mind your current life and choices:
- Whatever you are doing now is it leading to your aspirational life?
- Are you taking deliberate conscious actions towards your aspirational life or taking random actions, hoping to get it right?

- Are you taking steps to pursue your passion and what really matters to you in life?
- Are your current choices and actions aligned and contributing to your sense of fulfilment (leading to your aspirational life)?
- What you are doing currently, is it serving your life's purpose or just a doing it because you are required to?
- Are you being driven by circumstances, people, situation instead of your aspirations?
  Note: stick to one-word responses
- Review your responses and assess the level of alignment between your aspirational life and your reality

- What are you feeling (highlight the most common ones)?

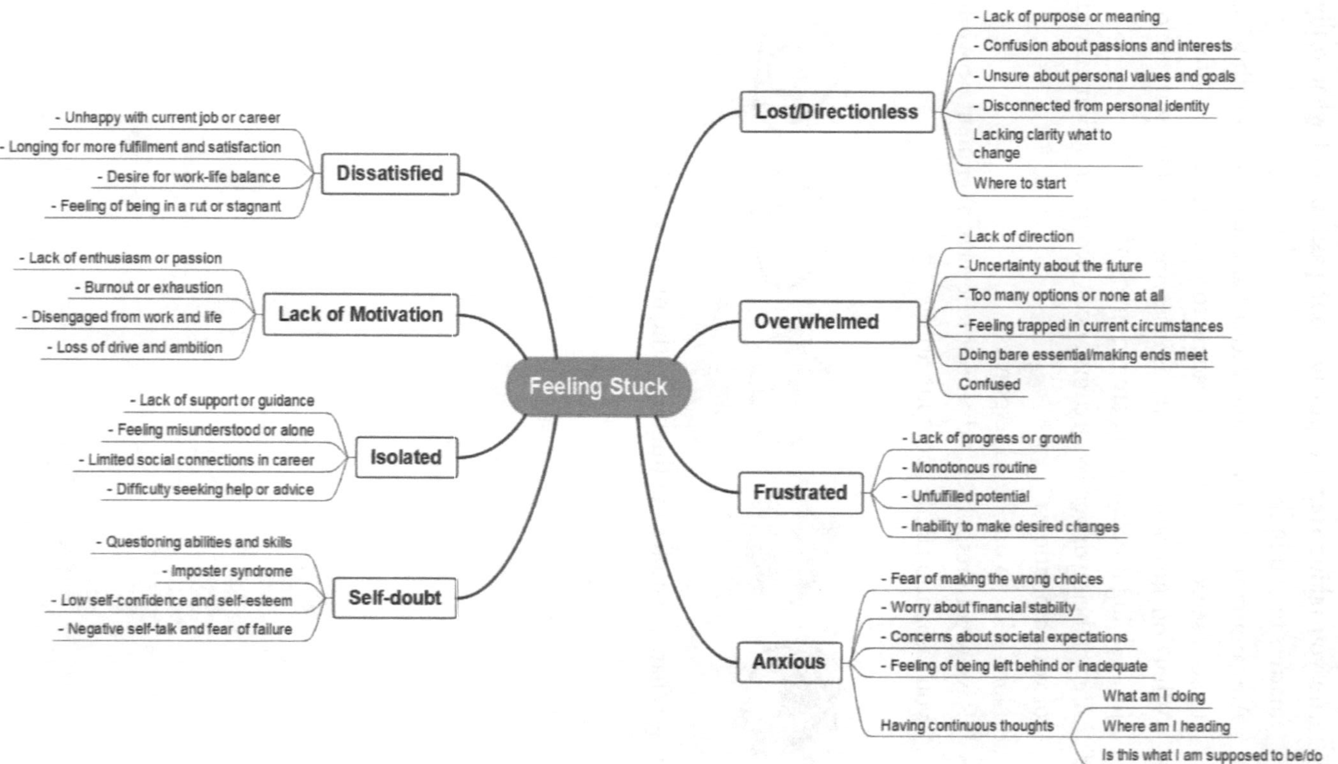
Feeling Stuck

Lost/Directionless
- Lack of purpose or meaning
- Confusion about passions and interests
- Unsure about personal values and goals
- Disconnected from personal identity
Lacking clarity what to change
Where to start

Overwhelmed
- Lack of direction
- Uncertainty about the future
- Too many options or none at all
- Feeling trapped in current circumstances
Doing bare essential/making ends meet
Confused

Frustrated
- Lack of progress or growth
- Monotonous routine
- Unfulfilled potential
- Inability to make desired changes

Anxious
- Fear of making the wrong choices
- Worry about financial stability
- Concerns about societal expectations
- Feeling of being left behind or inadequate
Having continuous thoughts
What am I doing
Where am I heading
Is this what I am supposed to be/do

Dissatisfied
- Unhappy with current job or career
- Longing for more fulfillment and satisfaction
- Desire for work-life balance
- Feeling of being in a rut or stagnant

Lack of Motivation
- Lack of enthusiasm or passion
- Burnout or exhaustion
- Disengaged from work and life
- Loss of drive and ambition

Isolated
- Lack of support or guidance
- Feeling misunderstood or alone
- Limited social connections in career
- Difficulty seeking help or advice

Self-doubt
- Questioning abilities and skills
- Imposter syndrome
- Low self-confidence and self-esteem
- Negative self-talk and fear of failure

If the answer to most of the assessment questions is "no," then I am sure you realize now that there is a misalignment between your Aspirations and Reality.

- Now, imagine how you would feel if it stays like this for years? Would you be content with material gains but still feeling stuck in a meaningless reality? Consider the consequences of not taking action towards your aspirations.
- What would motivate you to take the leap towards transforming your life right now?
- On a scale of 1 to 10, rate your commitment to taking action and aligning your life with your aspirations.

Your commitment level: ________

If your response is less than 9, then you are not ready as yet because you will not be motivated enough, your efforts will be inconsistent, you will easily get distracted and will not hold yourself accountable. What would it take to increase your commitment level to a 10?

I am sure you will say that "turning this situation around sounds like a pretty big deal!" Yes, indeed it is difficult but not mission impossible.

The best part about this is you don't have to jump in right away. Within these pages, you'll craft your personalized blueprint for success. It's about pulling out your plane from the parking bay and steering it onto the runway, all set for take-off.

Transformation or Change

Transformation or change, while they may appear similar, they carry distinct meanings and implications.

"Change" has been a prevalent keyword for ages, and the latest (or, rather not so latest), but relatively new is "Transformation."

Lately, the new buzzword is "Transformed." The real question is, are they the same or different? Well, they are different.

Change is primarily concerned with fixing things that did not work in the past; in specific areas of work or life, to correct past errors. Or working on a vision that may no longer be relevant.

Transformation entails redefining how things are done. It is future-focused. It is necessary to reconsider, assess, and redefine the current situation in light of future vision, as well as to align the execution with it. Its scope is much broader than merely fixing past mistakes. It's not about looking back and fixing what didn't work; it is about looking forward and shaping your present, revising your strategies and execution based on a future vision. The key is to maintain that future-focused mindset throughout the transformation journey. Well, the past isn't entirely irrelevant; you still have knowledge and experiences that can help.

Transformation occurs when one works toward a vision of the future, and all actions are directed toward making it a reality. Transformation is a continuous journey of self-discovery, growth, and evolution. It is a process of self-reflection, purposeful and intentional change, and ongoing learning.

The beautiful part is that while you are on this journey, you will discover things about yourself that you had no idea existed within you. Each step forward reveals something new about you.

Remember, it is not a linear process, and plans can and will fail; what matters is how committed you are to your journey of transformation.

Transformation necessitates a shift in attitude and behavior, and if your actions are not in line with what you want to achieve, your transformation journey will fail, resulting in frustration and loss of faith in the transformation process.

6 Strategies for Transformation

1. Set clear goals: Determine what you wish to achieve through this transformation. Gaining clarity will assist you in developing a plan of action.

2. Self-awareness: Explore and reflect on yourself like you've never done before. Engage in deep exploration and reflection of your values, beliefs, strengths, weaknesses, and shortcomings. This is the key to making intentional changes.

3. Cultivate mindfulness: It is critical that you are able to anchor yourself in the current moment. Develop a habit of being fully present in the moment, free from attachments and aversions. It allows you to easily navigate through the process effectively.

4. Continuous learning and improvement: Seek new experiences, knowledge, and skills to help you grow personally. This will broaden your horizon and empower your journey of transformation.

5. Take ACTIONS: There will be no transformation without actions. Break your goals into manageable milestones to avoid feeling overwhelmed. Remember, actions fuel transformation.

6. Persistence: Be consistent in your efforts. Things can and will go wrong, and you will make bad decisions, but what will carry you forward is your persistent effort. Adapt and improvise along the way.

While you cannot really undo what you have done or un-live the life you have lived, you have the power to control your future and make a better tomorrow for yourself. It's about transformation to be your best self by gaining clarity, overcoming obstacles by taking actions. It's like a coder starting from scratch to develop new software or a painter painting on a blank canvas.

When I talk about obstacles, most of the time the obstacles are within you, and we blame others, situations, or circumstances for not being able to overcome them.

Unlocking the Path to Fulfillment: From Conformity to Transformation

Surprisingly, approximately 80% of people never really set any goals for themselves. They live life as it comes.

Out of those remaining 20% who define their goals, a staggering 92% of them fail to achieve their goals.

Are you one of them?

Shockingly 98% of people will never fulfill their dreams.

Initially, these numbers looked huge and disagreeable, don't they? But as you observe people and yourself, the truth becomes apparent.

One of the best definitions of success that I have heard, as told by Earl Nightingale, is "Success is the progressive realization of a worthy ideal."

A select few fall into the category of being successful, happy, and fulfilled. They are the ones who define clear goals for themselves to live a purposeful life and are progressively working towards it. They are not different from you and me. They appear perfectly ordinary and similar to us, but they know what they are after, and they go for it. In contrast, for many of us, life unfolded as it did, different from the one we aspired or dreamt of.

Where do you think you are currently lying on this statistic? Are you part of the 98% who feel confused, stuck, and merely going with the flow? Or the elite 2%?

Reflect on your own life and determine where you believe you currently lie on that statistic.

- Pursuing higher education or a specific course because they are regarded as prestigious, even if they don't align with your true interests or aspirations.
- Setting goals that are easily attainable, rather than ambitious ones that push you to venture out of your comfort zone.
- Making professional decisions based on societal expectations or what others are doing, rather than following your true passion or interests.
- Adhering to societal norms and expectations without questioning their relevance or impact on your life.

- Making decisions based on what others believe to be correct rather than using your own judgment and values.
- Adhering to social media conventions, seeking validation through likes and followers.
- Adopting a particular lifestyle just for the sake of becoming popular or widely accepted, rather than what truly brings you happiness.

Being in that 98% is not so bad; it's not a negative thing in every situation. You are part of the crowd doing what everybody is doing, but it limits you and prevents you from being an authentic self. It may lead to success, but it often lacks fulfillment.

I chose some subjects in my senior secondary and completely different ones in graduation, and honestly, I did just fine. It's not that I loved it or hated it, but I did what was expected of me.

I was a bit of a wanderer back then, not knowing what I wanted to do, so I did whatever came my way, and it wasn't half bad! In fact, it turned out to be pretty fine. But there was always this little mischievous monkey inside of me, itching to try something new, something grander. I did well in my jobs, earned well, led a decent life so far. And, in certain ways, I'd say I was happy. But was I content? Maybe not. I had material possessions, but more than that, I desired that sense of accomplishing more than mere possessions.

Parents often tell their children to do courses that are the most popular ones, thinking that's what is good for them to be successful, without allowing them to explore their own interests and options. It's not like my parents were like that, but somehow I ended up doing it.

I did a Google search for "least taken up courses for graduation in India," and I got results like "10 most professional degree courses," "Best courses," etc., and guess what, it had those usual choices of courses like MBA, Engineering, Medicine, CA, Law, and many more. No doubt that doing these courses will land you in a good job, and yet I see so many people confused and stuck in their choices.

Imagine driving a car without a steering wheel. That's what a lot of us do. I don't mean it literally. The analogy of driving a car without a steering wheel serves as a metaphor for the lack of control most of us have over our lives. We may think we have control, yet deep down, we often make choices driven by external factors, influenced by fear, or self-perceived limitations. Conformity and complacency become patterns that hold us back.

In this metaphor, the car represents our life, and we are the driver, or at least we believe so. It symbolizes the choices, decisions, and actions we take to navigate our path and shape our destiny. However, for some of us, it feels as if we have limited control over our lives. We may find ourselves going through the motions, following the same routines, and being guided by external circumstances or expectations rather than actively steering our own course.

If you agree with this and upon self-reflection, you feel that you are in that same situation, then you are in that 98%. Would you want to move to the 2% class and live your dream life? Well, that's kind of a rhetorical question, but mostly we choose to stick with the familiar and go with the flow because it's comforting. It gives a sense of security and reduces uncertainty. Going with the flow will for sure get you things that make you happy, those fleeting moments of happiness. It might bring comfort and joy in the short term but will not lead to personal growth, exploration, or new experiences. It's a choice between finding momentary joy or seeking personal development.

I am sure you would say, "Yes, you want to transform," and at the same time, you wonder, "How?"

The fact is that many of us are feeling stuck, yearning for transformational change, imagining ourselves wanting to do something different than what we are doing.

"The biggest problem is not failure, but giving up even before making an attempt."

Some try, fail, and give up, while others do not even attempt to achieve their goals. Fear of daring goals, perceived challenges, or feeling overwhelmed by potential risks may discourage taking action. Overwhelmed by the potential risks and uncertainties, resulting in a lack of initiative or readiness to venture beyond their comfort zones. As a result, they merely accept what comes their way and are hesitant to take any additional steps toward fulfillment. Self-doubt and lack of confidence may cause people to doubt their abilities or worthiness, weakening their belief in their ability to succeed.

Say "Yes" if you agree with me

And if you agree with me, then you have accepted life as it is. The good news is that no matter which phase of life you are in, you can still transform it to how you want it to be. It starts with you acknowledging the fact and taking actions.

You might think it's clichéd advice, but the difference lies in how you approach it this time.

Remember, you hold the power to shape your life no matter what stage you are in. Take control, break free from conformity. After all, who's going to ask you how much time you invested to achieve the success you deserve? People around you will be more interested in the journey.

" *Victory begins in the playground of your mind before it's won on the field* "

Inner Boundaries and Obstacles

Over the years, we have become fixated on the idea that our current situation is the best we can have and have stopped trying to make a difference, thinking it's not worth the effort because of our mental blocks. Many of these blocks are often rooted in our past failures, hesitations to act, or those limiting beliefs that don't serve you well.

To break free from this mindset, it is essential to have clarity about who you are and not who you must be, and progressively work towards being your true self. You can't do it in one go; it's not a one-time event. You will have to make a consistent effort with dedication and make success a habit. When it becomes a habit, we yearn for more and more of it. It is addictive.

Uncertainty is perfectly normal, as it is part of life. After all, nature is uncertain. We can't control many things, but we can plan for the future and make informed decisions based on the best information we have available. In this case, not external information, but what's within. This is where this framework will help you gain clarity on self.

Choices do exist, but often, we choose to stick with the first or most obvious option that comes our way, thinking that this is the best there is or the options given to us by others. Well, that's not choosing; that's accepting or settling for whatever comes.

Take a moment to recall the first job that you landed in after completing your studies. Many of us might not have imagined ourselves in that role, but circumstances led us there, and we became comfortable with it, not exploring other options.

I never imagined myself doing a desk job, yet I found myself doing it for around 20 years. I aspired to follow in my father's footsteps (Wg. Cdr. AK Budhraja) as a pilot in the armed forces. I aimed for Army aviation but unfortunately didn't get through. The next best option was to join the private aviation sector, not as a pilot though, didn't have the finances. I did work for an airline operation for some time. I absolutely loved it. There are some memories that stick in your mind, and whenever you recall them, you remember every detail. This, and some others that I have and will be sharing going forward.

So, I was getting trained, and there I was standing in front of a commercial passenger aircraft. It was amazing; however, life took an unexpected turn, and I ended up in a desk job, which I believed was the only best option then, as I had never explored. All the while, the companies, salaries, and comforts improved annually. Whenever I felt that I was done with that company, there was another job with even better salary and perks waiting to be picked up.

The underlying sense of unfulfilled potential lingered within me. I deeply felt that there was more to life than this, and yet I was settling for the comfortable life I had. I was happy because all my needs were being met. However, comfort and happiness are not the same as fulfillment.

To me, fulfillment is when your life serves a purpose, and you are living the life you were meant to live, doing what you love, reaching your fullest potential. It's like you are where you should be by virtue of your authentic self. When you are in that place, both physically and metaphorically, that resonates with who you truly are, you are more likely to experience a deep sense of contentment and satisfaction. Living in accordance with your true self requires clarity about your aspirations, passion, purpose, and true potential.

Each one of us can do much more than what we think we can, yet we often choose to live a mediocre life, believing it to be the best option available.

You can be happy yet feel unfulfilled from within

Despite yearning for transformation, we often get fixated on self-perceived limited options and current circumstances, which can result in a sense of complacency and resignation. This situation, while offering familiarity and comfort, may not entirely correspond with our true aspirations or lead to genuine fulfillment. Hence, we keep persuading ourselves that this is the best there is, dismissing all the possibilities.

Each one of us possesses immense, yet untapped potential waiting to be harnessed. We hinder our growth by creating self-imposed boundaries and failing to take actions to overcome these impediments. Spending a lifetime living within those perceived boundaries and staying confined to our comfort zones prevents us from ever realizing the finest version of ourselves.

Speaking about these boundaries, they primarily exist within our minds. And, to justify them, we resort to making excuses. Excuses, not just to others but, most importantly, to ourselves. Excuses for not taking actions or stepping out of our comfort zone, for not following our passion.

Life with Excuses

Excuses may seem valid, but they keep us from realizing our full potential. Excuses like:

- "It's too late now" or "I'm too old to change things now" - 'It is never too late until it's too late,' and there is no point in this journey called life when it's too late to embark on a new path or make substantial changes unless you are unwilling to do so. Life is full of opportunities and chances for renewal. By embracing the change mindset and being willing to take action, we can create a life aligned with our true aspirations. In all honesty, answer this: By following the path and achieving your aspirational life, do you want to enjoy your dream life or waste time worrying about not getting here earlier? Besides, who's going to ask you, "Why so late?"

- "The time is not right" - New beginnings don't happen when the timings are right, and above all, new beginnings are seldom simple. To get to where you desire, you'd have to give up where you're currently headed, which only a few dare to do. We keep telling ourselves to wait for the right moment, an ideal setting for everything to fall in place before taking action. Even with the best of intentions and planning, things can and will go wrong. You must realize that there will always be uncertainties and risks, and you will only learn about them once you begin. Remember that life is full of uncertainty, and waiting for the perfect moment may not be possible, resulting in missed opportunities. Embrace the challenges, learn from setbacks, and seize the present moment to embark on a new beginning. It is through these courageous actions that we can create a life that aligns with our true desires and aspirations.

- "Don't know what I want" – This is actually quite common and stems from a lack of clarity because we never explore beyond the known. We confine ourselves to our known and comfortable zones, limiting our exposure to new experiences, perspectives, and opportunities. We become accustomed to the familiar and may feel hesitant or apprehensive about venturing into the unknown. This lack of exploration can result in a limited understanding of our own wants and desires. Intentional exploration and self-reflection can help us gain clarity on the path that aligns with our purpose and aspirations.

- "I am not sure if it's possible" - Grossly underestimating the immense potential we have and constantly undervaluing ourselves. It's important to reflect on past experiences when we have amazed ourselves by accomplishing something we never imagined we could do. These moments serve as powerful reminders of our capabilities and should motivate us to continue pushing our limits. Think back to a time when you surprised yourself with an achievement or accomplishment. Maybe it was learning a new skill, overcoming a difficult challenge, or accomplishing a goal that seemed out of reach. In those moments, you likely proved to yourself that you are capable of more than you initially believed. Having doubts and fears are natural human experiences. Fear is good as it keeps you at the height of your senses when you are trying something new, but it shouldn't hinder your progress in pursuing your aspirational life.

- "Don't know how" – One common excuse that often holds us back is the belief that we don't know how to achieve something. While it may be true that there is no set formula for success or reaching our goals, it's important to remember that many people have figured it out before us. There is no shame in seeking help and guidance from others, whether it's a friend, mentor, or coach. By seeking help, we gain access to a wealth of knowledge, expertise, and resources that can accelerate progress.

The fact is that each one of us is capable of coming up with our own solutions, but sometimes we need a push, a challenge, and support from someone other than ourselves.

In Western countries, almost everyone has a coach, including the most successful people like CEOs and managing directors. In fact, in India also, some of the most successful people that you see and hear about in the papers and news, have coaches.

These coaches don't hand out solutions, rather guide you to discover your own answers.

- "Won't make it" – Your limiting beliefs and biases ingrained in your mind are stopping you from achieving that life.

Last but not the least

- "Don't have time" – This is one of the most common and widely used excuses that I hear, and in fact, I myself am guilty of giving this excuse. We repeatedly tell ourselves and others that our lives are so busy that we can't find the time to pursue other endeavors. While it may seem true that time is limited, the reality is that we often make random choices without clear goals or a defined purpose, which consumes our time and leaves us wondering where it went.

Many of us fall into the trap of simply existing rather than thriving. We spend our days doing what we feel we must do to make ends meet, following routine tasks and obligations, without considering what truly brings us fulfillment. As a result, we become disconnected from our true self. Do you really want to live your life merely existing, doing what you must do, or thrive by doing what you want to do?

Just ask yourself these questions:
- Do you feel your life is happy, meaningful, fulfilled, and balanced?
- Given a choice, would you stick to the same life?

If the answers to each one are "No," then you know what to do. The choice is yours to make, whether it will be the status quo or your transformation.

CRISIS: ENERGY OR TIME?

In the midst of our busy lives, we often find ourselves consumed by worry, anxiety, and overthinking. Attempting to navigate through this chaotic mental state is like trying to sail a boat in a stormy sea. No matter how hard we row, the waves of worries and anxieties keep crashing upon us, leaving us feeling stuck, helpless, and completely drained of energy. To address this severe energy crisis, we need more than just a temporary boost like a Red Bull.

Just as a calm lake allows you to see the beauty of its surroundings clearly, a peaceful mind enables you to navigate life with focus and enthusiasm.

There's a severe energy crisis

The truth is, most of the time, we feel drained because we are stuck in life choices that may not resonate with us. Yet, we never explore beyond those choices.

Now, take a blank and fresh piece of paper. Seriously, take one.

Crumple it up and make a ball. Done?
This crushed paper represents our minds when we feel stuck, filled with multiple thoughts, opinions, anxieties, depressive thoughts, and fantasies. One thought leads to another, creating a self-reinforcing cycle of negativity. It keeps adding as we keep focusing on it.

Let's consider a scenario: You are working for a successful organization, and you have been working hard to get things rolling both professionally and personally. You are well-respected by colleagues, and overall, things are going well. However, the economy takes a turn, and the company undergoes some changes that may result in layoffs, but not yet.

What would be your reaction to this situation?
You will worry, right? You'll probably spend time researching the company's standing and financial status, and what the industry is saying about attrition in a similar industry. You will worry if you are one of those being laid off and if that happens, what will happen to the loans you have taken and your family, etc. You would worry about:

- Financial security: Losing a job would mean a sudden loss of income, which would impact the ability to support your family and yourself.
- Career stability: Finding a new job in a tough economy with increasing unemployment rates could be challenging and uncertain.
- Professional reputation: Being laid off could be perceived as a failure or reflect negatively on your work performance, potentially damaging your professional reputation.

- Lifestyle changes: Your job provides you with benefits, such as health insurance and retirement savings, which would also be impacted.
- Future prospects: The job market could be competitive, and it could take a long time to find a new job with similar benefits.
- Blah, blah, blah.

Seriously, life throws lemons at us, and what do we do? Focus on its sourness, why not mix up a refreshing cocktail with your favorite spirit? turning challenges into something enjoyable.

These concerns can cause greater anxiety, fear, and stress, creating a distorted perception of reality, fueling even more negative thoughts. Stuck in a loop, this cycle can make it difficult for individuals to break out of negative thinking patterns and can lead to increased stress and anxiety levels. As a result, instead of thinking about the positive aspects of their situation, individuals only focus on the worst-case scenarios. This biased and limited perspective further reinforces negative thinking patterns.

Similarly, someone who is constantly worried about their health may spiral into a cycle of fear and anxiety about potential illnesses and their impacts. This can result in being on a constant lookout for symptoms of illness, even if they are minor, leading to increased anxiety and fear. Additionally, there may be worry about going to the doctor and getting a diagnosis that confirms their worst fears. If diagnosed with an illness, they would worry about the treatments available and how it would impact their life, work, finances, and so on.

A decent level of worrying is good as it keeps you sharp. It is a natural survival tool that helps us respond to potential threats and dangers. If kept balanced and under control, it can be healthy and help you adapt to the situation, keeping you alert.

However, most of the time, it becomes excessive and takes over your thoughts and actions, leading to negative outcomes. It grapples you into endless loops of negative thinking, and before you know it, you spend your productive time worrying about things that may not be relevant. You waste your time on irrelevant thoughts and actions, such as endless internet searches and videos.

While we are in this state, we often fail to consider the alternative perspective.

Maybe the layoffs were a necessary adjustment by the company to optimize resources. Maybe it's time for you to reassess your career and explore possibilities to make yourself lay-off proof.

Perhaps the pain you are experiencing is simply a muscle stretch pain, or the persistent headache you are having is due to the anxiety associated with worrying about having a tumor, keeping you awake at night, and leading to internet searches that may validate your fears because you believe you have all the symptoms.

Research has shown that negative thinking activates neural pathways associated with stress, releasing stress hormones and triggering the "fight or flight" response. Repetitive negative thoughts can reinforce negative patterns, making them more automatic and harder to change. The brain's tendency to validate fears can create a self-reinforcing cycle, intensifying anxiety and worry.

Individuals who engage in repetitive negative thinking are more likely to experience symptoms of anxiety and depression, and they may also be at greater risk for developing these disorders. Negative thinking patterns can alter the structure and function of the brain over time, particularly in areas related to mood regulation and emotional processing. This can create a feedback loop where negative thinking reinforces itself, making it more difficult to break free from.

Additionally, the reason why the brain can get stuck in a negative thoughts loop is that it is constantly trying to seek information that supports existing thoughts and beliefs. When an individual has a fear, their brain may focus on the negative aspects of a situation and seek out information that confirms their fear, creating a self-reinforcing cycle where the fear leads to negative thinking, which then leads to increased anxiety and worry, and further negative thinking.

Thinking is a fundamental aspect of the human experience and plays a significant role in shaping our emotions, behavior, and mental health. In particular, negative thinking patterns, such as repetitive negative thoughts or worries, can have a profound impact on our mental and physical well-being. This manifests as mental, physical, and psychological issues, resulting in feelings of being stuck, lost, exhausted, directionless, overwhelmed, frustrated, and anxious.

However, it's not all doom and gloom. Positive thinking and mindfulness practices have shown to improve mental health and reduce anxiety and depression symptoms. Focusing on positive experiences and reframing negative thoughts can have a positive impact on our well-being.

Get more out of your mind

Objective: The objective of this activity is to gain insight into the thoughts that arise during specific tasks, situations, circumstances, and assess whether they are empowering or disempowering. By creating mind maps and identifying recurring patterns, triggers, and disempowering thoughts, you can develop a plan of action to remove or reframe them, allowing room for personal growth and enhanced productivity.

- Open your notebook or digital document, and at the top, write down the date, time, location, and the people you are with (if applicable). This will provide context for your reflections.
- Choose specific tasks or activities that you regularly engage with. Consider the goals you intend to achieve through each.
- Now, as you engage in each task, pay close attention to the thoughts that come to your mind. Be honest and open about what you think and feel during each activity.
- Create a mind map, connecting related thoughts and organizing them into different branches or categories. Use visual elements like arrows, keywords, and symbols to represent the connections between thoughts. Be as creative as you like!

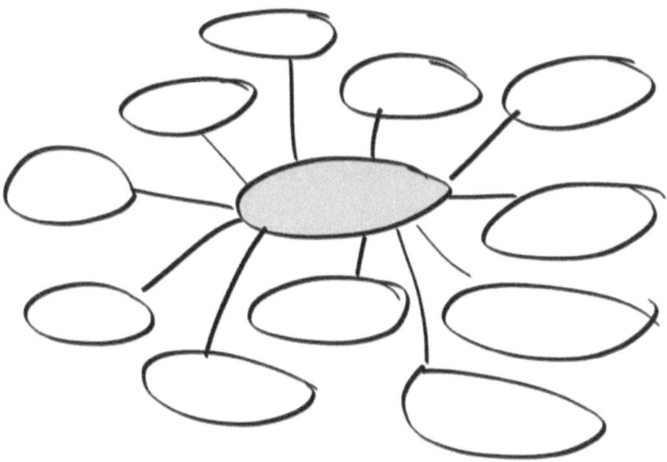

- How do you feel about those thoughts? What are the consequences? How do they impact the objective of the task and your well-being? Are they empowering and supportive of your goal, or are they disempowering and hindering your progress or causing negative emotions?
- Do this for several days and look for recurring patterns, triggers (such as time, place, people, location), and common disempowering thoughts.
- Review your mind map and observations. Look at insights or realizations that emerge from this analysis.
- Develop your plan of action. Set specific goals and actionable steps to remove or reframe the disempowering thoughts. Focus on cultivating empowering thoughts that align with your aspirations.
- Monitor your progress.

Detail	Tasks	Goal	Thoughts (mind map)	Consequences	Empowering or Disempowering	Plan of Action
(Time, location, people)						

What actually is the "Energy crisis," which we often justify as a "Time crisis"?

Obviously, how can we find time for anything else when we are preoccupied with irrelevant matters and trapped in unproductive thoughts and emotions? This drains us of all our energy. This energy crisis is internal to us, and most of us struggle with it on a daily basis.

However, what's amusing is that instead of confronting this internal crisis head-on, we often resort to justifying it as a time crisis. We frequently make excuses like "I don't have time," "It's too late now," or "I'm waiting for the right time."

By attributing our energy crisis to a shortage of time, we inadvertently avoid facing the root of the problem, which is our internal struggle. We create a façade, making it appear as though time is the culprit behind our lack of progress and fulfillment.

In doing so, we miss the opportunity to acknowledge and address the real issues at hand. We trap ourselves in a never-ending loop of procrastination and avoidance, further exacerbating our energy crisis.

Think about the last time you wanted to make a major change in your life. What happened? Were you able to make that change?

Now, reflect on your current actions and choices. Would your 10-year-old self feel proud of you or embarrassed? Are you genuinely happy, fulfilled, and satisfied with the path you have chosen, or are you simply following the expectations of others or the choices they have made for you?

If the answer is "NO," then you are squandering your energy by remaining stuck in this situation and constantly brooding over it. This frustration drains the energy out of you, preventing you from utilizing your immense potential.

It's your choice: either stick with the excuses and continue being the crushed paper, or spread it out, uncrumple it, and straighten it to start a whole new story. Immense possibilities will open up then and there. Imagine what you can do with that piece of paper - write a story or a poem, create a paper plane and fly it, craft a boat and sail it, or draw a masterpiece. Similarly, think about what you can do with your life.

Have you ever seen a rocket launch? I'm sure you have.

The rocket rises up because there is fire in its ass:), and so shall you rise if you ignite that fire within you for your launch to be the finest version of yourself.

Transformation through ACTIONS!

We are all born equal in terms of capability with certain exceptions, yet some can achieve their dreams while others don't. The difference is that those who have a clear vision about what they want and every step they take is aligned and supporting them towards achieving it. The most important thing is that they take actions and not just actions but focused actions.

So, the key to achieving what you want is:
- Clarity – Have a clear destination in mind and define your goals aligned with your passion and purpose to create a life you desire.
- Commitment – Dedicate yourself wholeheartedly to the process of achieving your dreams. Your life's journey is yours to shape; choose to make a difference by committing to taking actions.
- Focus – Stay focused on taking actions that are aligned with your life goals. While the outcome matters, we often make the mistake of getting fixated on the outcome and not living the journey. Remember, the journey is as important as the

destination. Focus on each step and the growth and learning it brings. Once you have the goals defined, focus on the next step to achieve that.

- Accountability – Take responsibility for your actions and inactions. Hold yourself accountable for the progress you make. Recognize that you have the power to shape your own life, and you and only you can make the difference.
- Consistency – Be consistent in your efforts. Understand that setbacks and obstacles are part of the journey. Embrace adaptability and improvise along the way. Consistent actions, even in the face of challenges, will lead you toward your goals.
- ACTIONS – Turn your ideas into tangible steps forward. Don't just think, act.

In addition to being the key to success, I consider these as values one should hold to achieve their desired reality.

I will be sharing this unique process of transformation through the ACTIONS framework. It's a journey of you designing your life through self-exploration and analysis. It is a process of gaining clarity, exploring possibilities, prototyping, and finally building the life that excites you, is meaningful, and is fulfilling. It's like a designer who builds things that don't exist, and of course, they do fail, but instead of dwelling on failure and getting stuck, they move on and try new options.

It will help you transform your life from what you "must be" to living your true self through exploration and designing your life how it's meant to be.

Transformational change necessitates deliberate and focused actions. You may have big dreams that appear audacious, difficult to achieve, and unrealistic. You may have tried and failed at some point in your life before giving up entirely. That resulted in you hesitating to take any further actions towards the fulfillment of those dreams because of the fear of failure, self-doubts, or lack of confidence. And you accepted the situation as it is. This time, let's do it differently.

"The solution is not to try harder but rather try differently," as stated by Anders Ericsson & Robert Pool in their book "Peak."

Purposeful practice is not about doing something repeatedly and expecting improvement; instead, it involves a well-defined and focused approach toward specific goals, gradually breaking free from the comfort zone.

Getting past each barrier that will come your way, you will gain confidence and the momentum to move forward toward the ultimate goal. And, by the way, throughout your journey, constant feedback, whether from others or through self-reflection, will be crucial.

The purpose of this book is to help you find your:

Why – Success demands clarity to define your life goals. Surprisingly, a substantial majority of individuals who don't fulfill their dreams lack a clear purpose in life? Their life is dictated by their habits stored in their subconscious mind. According to Duke University research, habits drive approximately 45% of our daily behaviors. This indicates that the majority of our actions are not made intentionally. Instead, we're merely following our habits, which impact every aspect of our life, whether it's relationships, career, wellbeing, etc. If your habits are not serving you well, it's time to change.

And, we have talked about our habit of procrastination, self-doubt, fear, feeling stuck, thinking, and overthinking.

Your "why" is your life's purpose, transcending mere career choices. It defines the direction of your life and who you are.

Without the knowledge and understanding of your "why," your "what" and "how" remain meaningless.

How – Transforming your reality involves exploring possibilities and gaining clarity to design your life options. It's about developing a blueprint with options that align with your purpose and your aspirational life, a well-defined plan of action involving a roadmap of actionable steps that will lead you toward becoming the best version of yourself.

As the saying goes, "We are what we think." Adopting a winning mindset is crucial to achieving your goals.

"Inside of me, there are two dogs. One is mean and evil, and the other is good, and they fight each other all the time. When asked which one wins, I answer, the one I feed the most."- Sitting Bull

What – Our life is about the options we choose and the ones we love. Your "what" is the life you've designed, a reflection of the choices you make. The aspirational or the desired life you shall achieve in alignment with your "why" and "how."

Options are available, yet we often fail to explore or overlook them, leading us to where we currently stand. Choices we make define the path we choose in life, and nothing could be worse than walking on a path that wasn't meant for us. Imagine wanting to reach destination "A," but the path we choose leads to destination "B," and upon arrival, you realize it's not what you were aiming for. Unlike computers, you can't simply reboot and restart instantly.

Options exist; some are hard, some easy, and some seem crazy. In all honesty, I would prefer the crazy ones; they are often the out-of-the-box ideas that excite, energize, and challenge me. Your destination is fixed, but the path to the destination is not. There are various ways to reach your destination, and it's all about choosing the one that resonates with who you are and is effective enough to reach your goal. The journey is only successful if the path you choose leads to where you want to be.

It's natural for things to go wrong, and ideas may fail, but that's okay. Failures are opportunities for learning and growth. Edison, despite his failures in studies, being home-schooled, doing odd jobs, and getting fired from his job, turned out to be one of the best innovators with over 1000 patents. Walt Disney had his share of failures too. He was fired for lacking creative imagination and was told he had no good ideas. He faced bankruptcy and had his ideas rejected multiple times. Despite all that, he was able to create what Walt Disney is today. Do you really think he lacked imagination?

You are who you are, but sometimes the environment, such as people, location, and timing, disrupts your flow. There are many such examples. Just imagine if Edison, Walt Disney, and many more like them had given up because of their failures as seen by others.

Life is uncertain, and you'll never know if an idea is good or bad unless you try it. Embrace experimentation and view each attempt as a step closer to your dream. And if it doesn't work out, don't worry; you are a step wiser.

When – come on! Seriously, do you need an answer to this? Actually, it's for you to decide. The average life expectancy of humans is 72.6 (according to the World Bank in 2021) years. Let's assume you will live up to that. Now subtract your age from 72.6. That's the number of years you have left to live. Even if it's less, you are still alive, right?

Ask yourself: Knowing that there's a choice, would you want to spend time from now feeling stuck and unfulfilled, or would you rather transform your life to live those years the way you were always meant to be?

The choice is simple. If you genuinely want to transform your life and create a better, more delightful tomorrow, you have to take action now. Remember this: all successful people have achieved their level of success by taking action and not by romanticizing about their ideal life. They weren't lucky, and opportunities didn't magically appear at their doorstep. They became successful by creating opportunities for themselves when they wanted them and by overcoming their mental barriers. Of course, they failed, not just once but multiple times, but that didn't stop them. They took action and remained consistent in their efforts. They didn't wait for directions; instead, they found their own path. Unlike many of us who say we will change our lives but keep waiting and doing nothing, successful individuals take action. They are not fearless;

in fact, they are just as afraid as the rest of us. The key difference is that they fear missing out on opportunities if they don't take action.

You don't have to hit rock bottom before realizing that you need to take action. You are here now, so why not start now? Even if you are doing well, ask yourself if your current situation aligns with your desired future. Sometimes, even after hitting rock bottom, we may still end up doing what we have to do rather than what we truly want to do. The universe provides us opportunities to be our best selves. How we utilize those opportunities makes all the difference.

If you have ever done gardening or planted a seed, you understand that what you put into the soil, whether a sapling or a seed, initially starts small and fragile. However, within it lies the potential to grow into a strong, towering tree. Nature provides everything needed for growth. Yet, not all seeds sprout and not all saplings become towering trees.

Similarly, within each one of us, there is the potential to grow and bridge the gap between what we are truly capable of and what we currently are. You have the choice to continue living with the same mindset that you've had, or you can choose to change it. Often, the major obstacles you face come more from within than externally, and you may experience failure at times. However, your persistence in trying again and again will eventually lead you to where you want to be.

As Maxwell Maltz said, "Within you right now is the power to do things you never dreamed possible. This power becomes available to you just as soon as you can change your beliefs."

Without exploration, there would be no discovery. Imagine if some of the things we take for granted, like electricity, the light bulb, or aircraft, hadn't been discovered at all. Life would be completely different. Similarly, you haven't fully discovered your true self yet.

Personally, through my exploration, I have discovered many things about myself, and this process is ongoing. In this journey, I have been amazed at the incredible things I could never have imagined doing.

- **Solo Paraglider Pilot:** I was always fascinated by the idea of flying. When becoming a fixed-wing plane pilot was not an option, I pursued the dream of flying by becoming a paraglider pilot. I enrolled in a paragliding course and learned the basics of flying. I gained more experience and confidence and embarked on solo flights, soaring through the skies with the wind beneath my wings.

- **Bike Rider:** At the age of 40, I discovered a love for biking and decided to buy a motorcycle. I had never owned a bike, but I used to ride my dad's scooter when I was young. I always had a liking for a bike, but never owned one, let alone ride it. So, here I was deciding to buy a bike, and instead of going for a normal bike, I went for an off-roader. My wife liked it too. I started with a few minor accidents and one slightly more significant, but that was part of learning. I began going for solo rides and then gradually ventured into off-roading on simple to challenging terrains. With each ride, my confidence grew, and I embraced the thrill of biking on and off-road. Lately, I have taken on the role of a mechanic as well, servicing and repairing my bike. I haven't become a pro or a super biker, nor do I intend to, but I am happy doing it.

- **Trainer:** I remember when I was in school and had to recite a story in front of the whole school. I ran away and hid when I was called. From a very young age, I was a shy and introverted kid. I never could imagine myself speaking in front of a large audience. Overcoming my shyness and introverted nature, I pushed myself to become a consultant and trainer, speaking in front of large audiences.

- **Marathon:** I challenged myself to run a marathon and ended up running a couple of them. Of course, I didn't win them, but I just wanted to not only take part in them but also to complete them. In one of them, I ended up running double the distance than what I had registered for. That was a funny story, maybe for some other time.

- **Living by Design:** Drawing from my transformative personal journey, I developed the 'Live by Design – Transformation Through ACTIONS!' program to inspire and guide others in exploring their potential and designing a fulfilling life. By creating a platform for self-exploration and personal growth, the program supports individuals in uncovering their passions, setting goals, and taking action towards their dreams.
- And there's more…

As I reflect on my journey and countless experiences, I realize that there is much more to discover and share. Each step, from conquering fears to embracing new challenges, has been a lesson in self-discovery.

"Journey never ends; destinations do."

The essence of self-exploration lies in the continual process of learning and growth, with endless possibilities waiting to be discovered and achieved. Reflecting on my own experiences serves as a testament to the fact that there is an untapped reservoir of potential within each person, waiting to be unleashed through exploration and action. A few years back, when I was in the corporate world, I was just working. I never could have imagined I had it all within me. I am not suggesting that there was no learning during my years in corporate; there was.

Let me assure you; self-exploration doesn't necessitate abandoning your current endeavors. The beauty of this process lies in its seamless integration with your existing life. By designing your path wisely, you can retain your hard-earned gains while uncovering unforeseen possibilities.

Many people are afraid of losing out or quitting what they are doing, and it is a valid fear. I realized this until I had no option, but you don't have to.

Through this book, you will explore yourself, and who knows that your own exploration in your life will take you where.

"Nothing is more expensive than a missed opportunity" — *H. Jackson Brown*

This book is for those who have embraced a certain career path, driven by conformity and a lack of clarity about their true passions and purpose. They yearn to explore other opportunities but struggle with stepping out of their comfort zone, procrastination, and self-doubt, making excuses such as "I don't have time" or "maybe tomorrow," and more. These individuals are constantly searching for more in life, yet they often find solace in what they have, buying material possessions in the hopes of finding contentment.

Their needs and challenges:

- They don't want to quit what they have because of the risk of losing it all.
- They are willing to explore themselves to gain clarity because they haven't really figured out what they want or what they are passionate about.
- They have been randomly picking up stuff, thinking that this is the one (actually again following others or imitating others), however, they lose interest because it's not.
- They lack support or feel that they will not get enough support.
- They want to be pushed out of their comfort zone.

As I delved deeper into this, I realized that individuals like my former self are everywhere. Individuals who are lost and continue with their daily tasks because they "have to" and not because they "want to". Many of them don't even acknowledge that they're stuck; instead, they keep trying new random things well within their comfort zones, in the hopes of filling the gap between what satisfies them and what they're doing now.

This leads to frustration, anxiety, feeling overwhelmed eventually at some point because they don't really explore who they are; instead, they simply follow a random path. Their frustration manifests itself differently.

Sam had worked in the IT field for many years, but he always felt like there was something lacking in his life. He picked this professional route because most of his peers and seniors were entering the IT sector, making it the most obvious alternative for earning a good living. He's never really known what he's actually passionate about. He wishes to pursue new opportunities, but he is terrified of taking risks and moving outside of his comfort zone. He frequently finds excuses for not following his aspirations and feels trapped in his current situation.

Sheila, a 35-year-old woman, is discontented with her current situation as a housewife. She opted to be in this predicament because it was what her family and society expected of her. She was never given the chance to discover her actual passions and purpose. She wishes to explore opportunities but finds it difficult to leave her current environment, so she procrastinates and makes excuses such as "I don't have time," "maybe tomorrow," and "this isn't how it's supposed to be." She continually convinces herself that this is how it is and will be. She wishes that she could get more out of life but compensates by purchasing material items and spending time with friends, in the hopes of finding happiness.

Many of us are trapped in tedious, unchallenging, and banal jobs or situations that wouldn't have been our first choice, but still happened because that was the obvious one. Some take action, and some accept and live in peace with their reality.

Which one are you?
"Life is like an endless highway. You will cross cities and towns; it's your choice to continue cruising on the highway or explore what comes along the way."

ACTIONS!

This is your transformational journey to be your best self, where you gain clarity, explore possibilities, and build a life that excites you, is meaningful, and is fulfilling. It is a unique program for transformation through ACTIONS.

While you are on this journey, you will work on your life goals and break them into short-term, achievable objectives, creating a habit of success as you progress on this journey. The objective is to take one step at a time and get closer to achieving a life that you are meant to live. Small wins make a significant difference towards achieving goals. As James Clear highlights in his book "Atomic Habits," these marginal improvements, seemingly insignificant day by day, compound over time, leading to significant positive changes.

Often, we define goals and become fixated on achieving them. Society ingrains in us the notion of setting a goal and working relentlessly to accomplish it. However, we rarely talk about the journey itself, which is just as crucial as the destination.

Consider weight reduction as a goal. While it is essential to eat healthily, exercise regularly, and stay disciplined, we often get caught up in obsessively checking the weighing scale, which can be demotivating. Instead, we should focus on enjoying every bit of success achieved along the way and learn from failures, adapting accordingly to stay on track.

Remember, your learning comes from the journey; failures help you adapt accordingly to stay on track. Not being on track doesn't mean that you have failed in your endeavor; it's just an obstacle.

Through this journey, I would like you to amaze yourself. You have it in you; you just haven't realized it yet.

Through the remainder of this book, I will take you through the ACTIONS framework. ACTIONS is an acronym for:

- **A**spire - Embrace the vision of becoming your best self, which includes unlocking your potential and achieving a life of fulfillment.

- **C**larity – Gain a clear understanding of your passions, purpose, and how they relate to your life aspirations. Define what truly drives and inspires you.

- **T**rue reality – Assess your current reality, acknowledging where you stand in terms of alignment with your desired reality. Recognize any gaps or areas of improvement to be addressed.

- **I**mpediments – Identify and explore the obstacles and challenges that hinder your progress toward the desired state. Develop strategies and techniques to effectively manage and overcome these impediments.

- **O**ptions – Explore possibilities and creative solutions in alignment with your passions and purpose. Different paths, roles, and opportunities that resonate with your aspirations.

- **N**OW – Take immediate action toward designing your ideal life. Implement the insights gained and make proactive choices that align with your passions and purpose, seizing opportunities in the present moment.
- **S**uccess – Celebrate each step forward and acknowledge your achievements along the way. Cultivate a mindset of continuous growth, recognizing that success is a series of milestones reached through deliberate and purposeful efforts.

Enjoy the journey; there will be other goals ahead

Instead of sleepwalking down this highway called life and making random decisions, embark on a journey of self-discovery. Explore your immense and yet underutilized potential. You don't have to go out into the world to find the answers; they are already within you.

Never stop being a daring life explorer. As Aristotle wisely said, *"Knowing yourself is the starting point for all wisdom."*

Create a well-designed blueprint of the life you are meant to live, one that is worthy of your life's calling.

Take the first step toward living your best life, and remember that self-discovery is like unwrapping a present—each layer reveals something wonderful!

Let's design…

A - ASPIRATIONS

Mindset

"Our capability is defined by what we think we can instead of what we really can."

People who prefer to stay within their comfort zone and believe that intelligence is fixed are said to have a fixed mindset.

On the other hand, individuals with a growth mindset believe that intelligence can be substantially improved. They are the ones who are happy to stretch their limits over and beyond their experiences. As you raise the complexity of the task, those with a growth mindset embrace the challenges and are happy to learn from it. They view it as an opportunity and are forever ready to learn, even if they know that the task at hand is beyond their capability.

Our potential is boundless, and each one of us is capable of doing and achieving much more than what we think we can, but we often impose limitations on ourselves.

People with a fixed mindset:
1. Feel a sense of urgency to succeed and derive immense pride when they do.
2. Tend to make excuses when they fail.
3. Ruminate on setbacks and failures, attributing them to personal incompetence, rather than taking corrective action.
4. Fear making an effort when faced with tasks beyond their current level.

The good news is that mindsets are not permanent; they can evolve and change with conscious effort and self-awareness through:

1. Awareness of two mindsets.
2. Reacting differently to situations, such as embracing challenges instead of avoiding, focus on learning and development instead of fearing failure.

It may be possible that you are in a growth mindset in one situation and fixed in another. Awareness of your mindset can help you change it. For example, "I'm not a math person" when it comes to math; this is the thought I get, and I steer away from that situation. At the same time, I am open to experimenting and learning different things (except math's off-course). I have a fixed mindset when it comes to math and a growth mindset when it comes to experimenting with new stuff.

There have been numerous examples of individuals with a growth mindset who embraced failures as part of the learning process to achieve remarkable feats and contribute to significant advancements in various fields. They see challenges as stepping stones to progress and are not afraid to take calculated risks.

In contrast, individuals with a fixed mindset fear taking risks and stepping out of their comfort zone. They may believe that their current strategies and methods have brought them success and may be reluctant to explore different avenues for fear of failure. They may resist adopting new technologies, processes, or innovations in their industry, assuming that what has worked so far will continue to be successful. They may be successful in achieving significant accomplishments, but their fixed mindset prevents them from reaching their full potential and exploring new opportunities.

An example of a visionary with a growth mindset is Dr. A.P.J. Abdul Kalam, the former President of India. He had a very humble beginning and faced a lot of challenges, yet he played a pivotal role in India's space and missile development programs and was instrumental in the successful development of ballistic missile technology. He saw failure as an opportunity to learn and grow.

"Dream is not that which you see while sleeping; it is something that does not let you sleep." — A.P.J. Abdul Kalam

Your mindset is your attitude towards life. A negative mindset limits your possibilities, while a positive one seeks solutions and adapts to challenges. It plays a pivotal role in determining your success. If you believe that you are too old or not skilled enough to transform your life, those are just excuses coming out of your fixed mindset. The truth is, as long as you are alive, you still have the power to transform your life. All it takes is having the right mindset and accepting the challenge of transforming yourself into a new version, and it doesn't matter where you are right now.

If given the choice, would you want to stick with the obvious or be willing to explore?

Beyond Grades

Do you think success only comes to smart, intellectual people, and that failure makes you a failure forever? It's a misconception to believe that success is only reserved for smart, intellectual individuals and that failure defines you forever. Also, being smart is contextual. I could be academically smart but artistically less skilled, but if that is relevant, then I could develop that as well with time. So, there's no point in judging smartness on flat criteria as we often do.

This brings back memories of my time in school when a student's intelligence was determined by how well they performed on their exams. Many successful individuals struggled in school or college. Richard Branson, who was dyslexic, left school when he was 16. According to Branson, "On one of my last days at school, the headmaster informed me that I would either wind up in prison or become a millionaire."

We have all seen the pressure, the pressure to do more, study hard, otherwise, you will not get a good college, then get good grades in college, or you will not get a good job, and so on and so forth. There has been and still is immense pressure from society and parents to do well academically. But in reality, we have seen that grades are not something that will define your success when it comes to it. Yes, they are definitely important for maybe getting a good start or a job, but once that is achieved, then it's a level playing field thereafter, where no grades will matter, but your mindset will.

I have never been a studious guy, yet I have worked with individuals coming out of the best business schools, and my opinions, suggestions, and work have been equally valued as theirs, sometimes even better. In fact, sometimes someone who is well-read and academically accomplished may struggle in a real-world scenario because they have spent too much time studying books than experiencing reality.

Grades do not define our success. The determining factor is our mindset. According to Carol Dweck, the author of "Mindset," our mindset significantly influences our achievements and success. We all face challenges in our daily life, but it's our mindset that helps us cope with these challenges. These beliefs are powerful enough to impact our successes or failures in life.

What's your story?

Honestly acknowledging your present reality without judgment or denial involves a sincere assessment of where you currently stand in various aspects of your life – relationships, career, health, personal growth, and well-being.

Avoiding reality can lead to complacency or a false sense of security, hindering your personal growth and potential. On the other hand, accepting your current reality with an open mind sets the stage for creating a plan to bridge the gap between your aspirations and your present situation. This self-awareness is crucial for making informed decisions and taking intentional steps toward your goals.

Your Aspirational Life:

The vision you hold for your future self. It is a compelling and inspiring picture of the person you want to become, the achievements you wish to attain, and the impact you desire to make on the world. Aspirations transcend the limitations of your current circumstances and propel you toward growth and self-fulfillment.

Your aspirational life should excite and motivate you to take purposeful steps toward realizing that vision. Aspirations are your vision of the future or an overarching striving.

Close your eyes and imagine yourself doing similar things to what you are doing now in five years, except that you have grown in designation and salary. Would you be happy and fulfilled?

Your Vision of the Future, Your True North:

Aspirations are the seeds of potential that reside within you. They represent your deepest desires and the path to living a fulfilling and purpose-driven life doing what you love doing. Your vision of the future serves as an expression of these aspirations—a clear and vivid picture of the life you wish to create for yourself.

This vision provides a sense of direction, giving meaning to your actions and decisions. It acts as your true north, a constant reference point, guiding and motivating you to take action. During challenging times, it fuels your motivation and inspires perseverance toward realizing your dreams.

Embracing your aspirations and actively working toward them brings a profound sense of fulfillment, empowering you to design the life you genuinely desire.

It's like having a compass in an unexplored land—your aspirations serve as this compass, helping you maintain alignment with your true desires. They provide focus, aiding you in making the right decisions to ensure that each step you take is on the correct path, in alignment with the finest version of your future self.

However, simply having a vision is not enough. Aspirations are powerful motivators, and achieving them necessitates commitment, consistent action, a willingness to learn, and making prompt course corrections when required. It requires the courage to take risks and make intentional choices. Without these, aspirations merely remain fantasies.

"A dream without committed and consistent actions to fulfill it remains a dream."

It's not enough to dream; you must act to turn those dreams into reality

"Before doing something special, you have to start by doing something."

Your vision will serve as a guiding principle and will inspire and motivate you along the way, keeping you focused and determined. It gives your life purpose, a sense of direction, and helps you stay focused on what truly matters to you. Having an aspiration means having something to strive for, something to work toward, and something that gives your life meaning. Remember that our aspirations are unique to us, and it is never too late to follow them.

Following our passions and pursuing what brings us joy is what truly defines success and happiness in life. It allows us to challenge ourselves and push our limits, helping us to grow and develop as individuals. It also gives us a sense of purpose and fulfillment, knowing that we are working toward something that we truly care about.

"Do not lose hold of your dreams and aspirations. For if you do, you may still exist, but you have ceased to live" Henry David Thoreau

Life presents us with dreams and aspirations, but the sad truth is that many people lose sight of these dreams as they grow up and encounter the realities of life. Societal pressure, parental expectations, and the pursuit of financial stability often lead individuals to pursue careers that may not bring them fulfillment or joy.

This narrow definition of success, perpetuated by schools, parents, and the media, can cause people to believe they have failed if they do not follow the standard path of success, which may include giving up on their dreams. This is why some professional courses become the go-to choice for many.

The emphasis on science and commerce over arts and creativity perpetuates the belief that these subjects are more important and valuable than others. This leads to a lack of recognition and support for individuals who have excelled in creative fields, further perpetuating the notion that these fields are not valuable or significant.

This mindset has been deeply ingrained in our society, where success is defined by the profession one chooses and the accumulation of materialistic possessions. Doctors, engineers, and lawyers are considered to be the epitome of success, while creativity and the arts are often disregarded and undervalued.

In truth, success is subjective and varies from person to person. What may bring fulfillment and happiness to one person may not be the same for another.

Excerpts of a coaching conversation (edited, of course):

Me: "What does success mean to you?"

Individual: "Having a lot of money, a high-ranking job, a big house, and being recognized as the best in my field. I want to outshine my peers."

Me: "What does having all of this bring to you, and where does it end?"

Individual: "It makes me feel important and respected. It would give me a sense of security and the freedom to do whatever I want. I guess it doesn't."

Me: "Do you get to do what you want?"

Individual: "No! I don't get the time to do anything else."

Me: "If that's the case, then why do you still do it?"

Individual: "I guess because I have to, and I don't know what else."

Me: "What fulfills you at a deeper level?"

Individual: "I guess I have never thought in that way. I have always defined success as measured by all."

Me: "Any moment you could recollect when you felt fulfilled and content, irrespective of the money or where you are in comparison with others?"

Individual: "Now that you are mentioning it, I feel really good when I am helping someone, contributing to a cause I care about, mentoring others in my field of work." Note: the response didn't come so easily

Me: "Sounds like there's more to your sense of purpose than just money and status. Can you incorporate more of the factors of fulfillment into your life?"

Individual: "Will explore this further."

To break free from societal norms, we must change our perceptions of success and recognize the importance of following our dreams and what fulfills us. Embracing our individuality, pursuing our passion and purpose can lead to a truly fulfilling life. However, this shift in mindset is not going to be easy, as societal norms are deeply ingrained in our culture. It takes courage to break free from these expectations and pursue our own path, but in the end, it is a reward worth fighting for.

Have you seen a seed and the power it holds within it? A seed holds incredible power and potential within them. They are nature's gift that carries the blueprint for life and growth. When a seed is planted, it has the ability to transform into a majestic tree, offering us numerous benefits and blessings. These benefits include shielding us from the scorching heat of the sun, releasing oxygen into the air, cleansing and purifying our environment and our homes, and absorbing carbon dioxide, among others.

This tiny seed contains everything it needs to become a flourishing and magnificent tree, which is where its true potential lies. It carries the genetic information, nutrients, and energy required for its growth. With the right conditions, such as sunlight, water, and fertile soil, the seed begins its journey. It absorbs nutrients from the soil, utilizes sunlight, and slowly extends its roots deeper into the earth. As time goes by and using nature's resources, it grows to be a tall tree, with branches and leaves reaching out towards the sky.

But all of these remarkable gifts would not be possible had the seed remained dormant or not been planted in the right conditions, exposed to harsh conditions. The world would miss out on all the benefits that trees bring to our lives.

If you want to grow, flourish, and live up to your potential, you have to sow the seed of greatness within you. Start by visualizing your aspirational life. It's like sowing a seed in the fertile soil of your mind. Your aspirations hold the potential to shape your future and bring that vision to life.

Within you, you have all that is required to grow, the potential to bridge the gap between your current capabilities and your aspirational self. However, like a seed, this potential requires nurturing and care to grow and blossom.

You need to see it first to believe in it and take consistent actions to make it a reality. Taking action is like providing the seed with the right conditions to sprout and grow. It's the moment you shift gears and put your aspirations into motion.

Remember that the journey from aspiration to fulfillment requires patience, persistent efforts, and resilience.

Life's aspirations vs. Materialistic Desires

It's important that you do not confuse your life's aspirations with materialistic desires such as owning a luxurious house or accumulating wealth, etc. While these may bring you temporary happiness, it will only last a couple of days or at most months, eventually leading to the pursuit of more desires. They do not provide lasting fulfillment. It's a vicious circle, and pursuing materialistic desires will be a never-ending rat race, as the desire for more and better never ceases.

Happiness is not solely dependent on acquiring possessions like a car or a mansion by the beach. It is about finding balance, prioritizing what truly matters to us, and taking deliberate actions towards those priorities. It involves nurturing relationships, pursuing meaningful experiences, and contributing to something greater than ourselves.

This happiness will come from within, not from external sources.

The transformation we seek is to shift away from the unending pursuit of materialistic things and focus on personal growth, fulfillment, and true happiness. It's all about designing your life that works for you and you only. It requires introspection and self-awareness. It requires us to take the time to reflect on our values, interests, and passions. By aligning our actions with these core aspects of ourselves, we create a life that brings genuine joy and fulfillment.

To fulfill your aspirations, live your purpose, and find happiness and fulfillment, it is important to reassess and make changes. Take some time to reflect on the following questions and write down your responses. This exercise will help you assess your current situation and explore whether your life's path aligns with your true aspirations and purpose.

- What is your intent?
- Are you living your life's purpose or following the expectations and desires of others? Reflect on your life's direction and consider whether you are living your life's purpose or simply following the expectations and desires of others. Write down your thoughts on how your current path aligns or doesn't align with your true aspirations and values. Note: it's okay if you are not clear with your purpose now. We will get to that later.
- Are you living up to your full potential? Are you continuously learning and growing personally and professionally? Are you

deeply engaged or absorbed in tasks that give you a sense of accomplishment? Do you feel content and have belief in your capabilities? Do you embrace challenges and setbacks? If your answer is "No," take some time to identify where and how you might be falling short. Explore areas where you can grow, develop new skills, or make changes to unleash your full potential.

- Are you doing something that fulfills you? Hints: What you are doing matters to you and instinctively feels good. You feel content within.

- Now, think about what you do and describe it. Write down the first thoughts that come to your mind. This exercise is important as it helps you assess your current situation.

Now, ask yourself if you have described what you do in a way that reflects a deeper purpose and contribution to others' lives or if it resembles a job description.

For example, if you are a doctor working in a renowned hospital, specializing in oncology and providing medical care to patients, your initial response might be:

"I am a doctor in a renowned hospital, specializing in oncology, diagnosing and treating patients with cancer."

Or

"I am a healer, dedicated to making a difference in the lives of individuals fighting cancer. I use my medical expertise to provide accurate diagnoses, develop personalized treatment plans, and offer compassionate care and support throughout their journey to recovery. I am committed to helping my patients regain hope, resilience, and a sense of normalcy in the face of adversity."

Usually, it's the former one.

Actually, had your response been the latter one, it would mean that you are passionate about your work. You don't work to live; rather, you love to work. It comes from the heart, and it's not robotic. The main point to consider is whether you feel that you are actually serving a purpose instead of following a routine.

Consider whether you are serving a purpose in your current role or if it's time to transform it so that it brings you joy and fulfillment. Remember that life is too short to spend it doing something that does not align with your passions and purpose.

- Finally, does your current path align with your aspirations and provide an opportunity for personal and professional growth?

Aspirations are not Goals

Aspirations represent visions of the future or overarching strivings that give direction to our lives. They represent our long-term desires and dreams of the life we want to live, driven by passion, values, and a sense of meaning. Aspirations focus on an ideal vision of the future.

On the other hand, goals act as the stepping stones and action plans that contribute to the fulfillment of those aspirations. Goals are SMART (Specific, Measurable, Achievable, Relevant, and Time-Bound) actionable steps that focus on the "how" aspect of achieving our aspirations. Goals provide focus, clarity, and a sense of achievement as we progress through them toward the larger vision.

Consider my vision of the future: My vision for an aspirational life is one filled with happiness and fulfillment. It involves living a life where I can make a significant impact on others, witnessing their growth and transformation as they tap into their immense potential. I envision a life where I continuously learn, grow, and contribute. Additionally, the envisioned life provides me with sufficient support to pursue the life I wish to lead and other interests.

To turn this aspiration into reality, several goals ("how") can be identified:

- Gain clarity on what I like and what serves a cause that I associate with.
- Assess where I am in relation to where I want to be.

- Understand and manage obstacles.
- Design life options.
- Gain experience.
- Create a plan of action to make it a reality.

Each goal represents a milestone, and achieving each goal will bring you closer to your destination. Note: These goals can be broken down further into sub-goals to provide a clear roadmap for progress and achievement.

What's Your Story?

Discover Your Aspirational Journey: A Vision Board Exercise

You are here…

Take a moment to reflect on your current reality and your dreams for the future. Write down your responses to the following questions. Be honest and introspective in your answers. This simple and engaging exercise will help you identify areas where you feel stuck and assess your motivation and commitment to transform your life.

- Current reality "As Is": Describe your life as it is right now. Consider various aspects like career, relationships, health, personal growth, finance, love, social life, and fulfillment. You can do this collectively including all the aspects or do separately for individual aspects. Be specific and honest about where you are right now. You may consider the following while describing your reality:
  - Career: Your current job or profession, level of satisfaction from the career path and the work you're doing, progression toward your professional goals, and whether your skills and talents are being utilized to their fullest potential in the role.
  - Relationships: Your relationships with family and friends, nurturing meaningful connections, spending quality time with loved ones, and the level of support they provide in your endeavors and understanding.

- Love and Romance: Your current romantic relationship or dating life, emotional fulfillment and connection, expectations and boundaries, and the level of understanding and support.
- Social Life: Social engagement, including social activities and spending time with friends, the quality and depth of your social interactions, and your sense of belonging and enjoyment.
- Health: Your overall well-being, including emotional, mental and physical health, active engagement in regular exercise, maintaining a balanced diet, and any health concerns or habits that need to change.
- Personal Growth: Pursuing opportunities for learning and self-development, personal goals for growth and development, and challenging yourself to step out of your comfort zone.
- Finance: Satisfaction with your current financial situation, including income, expenses, and savings, financial stability, and planning for the future aligned with financial goals.
- Fulfillment: Your sense of purpose and meaning in your daily life, activities or experiences that bring joy and satisfaction, and your sense of accomplishment and pride in your achievements.

- Based on your responses, describe your life story.

What's your story?

- Now, describe your story in one word: Sum up your life's story in a single word that captures its essence.

- Aspirational Life – "To Be" = vision of the future or overarching striving. Describe your aspirational life, keeping in mind that aspirations are not goals.
- Close your eyes and imagine yourself five years from now, living your ideal life. Focus on the impact of your actions and the positive changes around you.

How do you see yourself?

What do you see around you?

How do you feel?

Remember to picture what you see around you rather than what you are doing. I'm not interested in the job/work you are doing at that moment, only the impact of what you are doing, in your life and surrounding.

- Vision Board: Create a vision board canvas for your future self. Use images, drawings, or words to represent the life you aspire to live. You can also use cut-out pictures. Envision how you see yourself, the people around you, the places you are in, and the feelings you experience.

To achieve your aspirational life, remember these three aspects:

See it: Imagine and visualize your future possible self. Create a picture of your future possible self. Place the vision board where you can regularly see it.

Believe it: Have faith in your vision and believe in your capabilities to make it possible.

Act on it: Take action before doubts, anxiety, frustration, or overthinking take over. Work on reworking and reframing limiting beliefs and biases that may be holding you back (we will address this later).

- Evaluate each aspect of your life and assess whether they align with your aspirational life. Consider the following aspects:
- Love: Concentrate on your primary intimate relationships.
- Relations: Includes family.
- Social: Reflect on your social circle including friends.
- Health: This includes emotional, mental, and physical well-being.
- Career: Focus on your primary occupation.
- Finance: Assess your current financial status, including investments and savings.
- Growth and Development: Think about your personal growth and development.

- Recreation: Consider stress-busting activities you may be involved in.
- Spirituality: Reflect on your sense of connection to something bigger than yourself.

Identify which aspects are supporting your progress toward your aspirational life and which are hindering it.

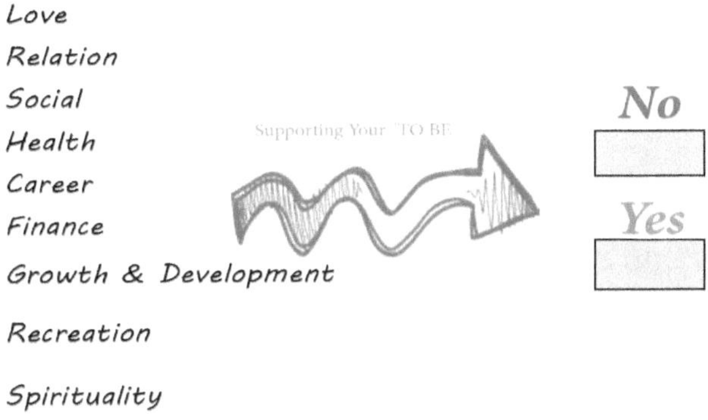

What's stopping you from living your desired "To Be' reality?	
Supporting	**Hindering**

The purpose of this exercise is to perform a dipstick check on where you currently stand in all aspects of life and make them work in our favor for progress. Understand that you can't tackle everything at once, so you need to prioritize the areas that require immediate attention. Keep in mind that we are taking one step at a time.

The journey toward fulfilling your aspirations can be likened to a road trip. Having an aspiration is like putting your car in "Drive," setting the wheels in motion, and giving yourself direction. However, just like a car, your aspirations require fuel to keep moving forward. Commitment is the fuel that propels you forward. Without it, your aspirations will remain stagnant.

The amount of fuel you invest in it will determine how far you go. If you put in a lot of effort and dedication, you will see results and achieve your aspirations.

So, set your aspirations, put your car in drive, and never stop pushing the accelerator toward your dreams. And remember, always keep the fuel of commitment and effort topped up.

Wholesome Happiness:

Happiness is about achieving balance and emphasizing what actually matters to us, not about financial rewards. It involves establishing equilibrium in all elements of your life (love, relationships, social, health, career, finance, growth & development, recreation).

This balance is crucial for overall happiness and well-being. When all aspects of our life are thriving, we are able to pursue our passions and aspirations with ease and joy. Conversely, if one aspect of our life is suffering, it can significantly impact our happiness and overall well-being.

Wholesome happiness is a journey that requires being intentional and thoughtful in all aspects of our lives. It's about making decisions that are in our best interests and align with our values. Prioritizing self-care, developing meaningful connections, and pursuing our hobbies and aspirations can all contribute to this.

Just like a well-maintained car with all its components working in harmony provides a comfortable and reliable journey, wholesome happiness is about being in tune with ourselves and our surroundings, leading a life that provides us satisfaction and contentment in all areas of our lives.

Without action, your aspirations are merely the status quo

Taking action is like providing the seed with the right conditions to sprout and grow. It's the moment you shift gears and put your aspirations into motion to propel them forward. Without action, your aspirations remain stagnant, mere ideas floating in your mind.

Without aspirations your actions lack directions

What do you do before you embark on a journey? Among other preparations, one of the most critical things is to have a destination in mind, right?

Without a destination, eventually, you will be wandering aimlessly, drifting wherever the wind takes you, and ultimately ending up nowhere. Similarly, engaging in random actions without a clear vision can lead to stagnation and a lack of progress. You will get somewhere, but not where you ought to be.

If you want to live a life of a wanderer, then that's exactly what you need to do. But answer this, isn't that what a lot of us are already doing—living life without any clarity of goals? How is it any different from what it is now?

To truly manifest your aspirations, it is important for you to have a vision to start with, a life that you eventually want to build for yourself. This would require a willingness to step outside of your comfort zone.

Aspirations are dynamic and ever-evolving. Reaching our aspirational state does not necessarily mean that it is the end of the journey. As we progress and reach our goals, we will be gaining new experiences and perspectives. While it is essential to have a clear vision and strive towards it, we must also remain flexible and open to change. Life is full of unexpected twists and turns, and our aspirations may transform as we mature and gain a deeper understanding of ourselves and the world around us. Embracing change and being adaptable allows us to seize new opportunities and redefine our path.

Many years ago, my ambition centered on being a data analyst. As I pursued that, it evolved into becoming a continuous improvement methodologies expert, driving improvement projects. This was followed by becoming a coach, mentor, and trainer to share my experience and knowledge, not just in quality but beyond as well, and that's how I developed the ACTIONS framework. Currently, my focus is on driving transformation and continuous improvement pursuing higher level of growth with focus on achieving performance excellence using proven methodologies and framework in driving people and operational excellence. I have not regressed; I have simply evolved.

Our aspirations may evolve as we grow and mature, and that is perfectly okay. Be open to re-evaluating and redefining it. What matters is that we continue to have a vision for ourselves and remain true to our values and beliefs that support our vision.

C - CLARITY

Human potential is vast and often remains hidden, waiting to be discovered. Many never realize their true potential simply because they haven't taken the time to explore themselves and unleash their true abilities. As a result, they settle for less. For instance, imagine someone who has a natural talent for creating music. She may have dedicated herself to honing this skill and deeply connects with music. However, despite her talent and passion, she might find herself trapped in the confines of the corporate world, never believing in her talent and exploring her passion for music.

Success requires clarity, a clear understanding of one's passion and purpose. They are the driving forces that propel individuals forward, and it is vital to gain clarity about both.

When we are fueled by a sense of purpose and driven by passion, we are more likely to achieve our dreams and aspirations. Purpose serves as a guiding light, directing passionate choices and actions toward a fulfilling life.

Imagine waking up early, stepping into your car, and commencing a journey. What's there to imagine? Most of you would already be doing that.

How about instead of the usual route, you embark on a journey without a defined destination, like a wanderer? Some might like the idea, and within those "some," very few or merely a handful could actually relate to this. But for most others, like you and me, how far do you think we would continue like this? The next block, the next intersection, the next town, the next city, or state? I bet you will stop at the next intersection, recognizing the impracticality of the idea. With the exception of a rare few, this notion is indeed unrealistic.

As outlandish as it might seem to many, it mirrors the lack of clarity regarding your passions and purpose, or the absence of understanding the "why" and "how."

Certainly, for a little while, you may enjoy the view. You may feel good about doing it or exhilarated about the prospect of doing something new—wandering from one place to another without any specific destination and purpose. Driven by a sense of adventure, curiosity, and a desire for self-discovery. However, it fails to reflect your true identity. The majority of us are not content with the concept of aimless wandering. We crave a sense of purpose, something to pursue that challenges us, imparts meaning to our lives, and shapes our essence.

Consider a straightforward test of whether you're a wanderer: If you would typically opt for a travel book over this one, have vague plans for the future, and exhibit instability (hopping jobs, relationships, fleeting interests), it's an indication. Here's a catch: even if you are not a wanderer, yet you are feeling stuck, overwhelmed, and restless.

Are you, in essence, running without any destination? In reality, there is a destination—often described as "living a good life." But do we genuinely comprehend what this entails or how to attain it?

"Having a good life" is a reasonable life aspiration, which often revolves around acquiring material possessions such as money, houses, cars, and an extravagant lifestyle. In pursuit of these desires, we are willing to slog relentlessly wherever we are, slogging in the workplace, slogging in relationships, harboring hopes of eventually attaining that "good life" in the long run. As you navigate this path, feeling trapped and discontented, you might transition from one job or relationship to the next, in search of something better. Yet, even after reaching the destination of wealth, fame, and possessions, why does the quest for more persist?

Over time, the majority of us have been driven by this desire, even as the components of a "good life" have evolved—from basic to higher needs. However, the essence of the pursuit has rarely revolved around leading a purpose-driven, fulfilling life.

Maslow's hierarchy of needs suggests that human beings are motivated by a series of needs arranged in a hierarchical order. According to this theory, individuals progress through these needs in a sequential manner, with each need serving as a foundation for the next level. When one need is fulfilled, we are motivated to move toward fulfilling the next one, starting from basic survival and ending at growth and self-actualization.

Yet, most of us often prioritize societal expectations, money, and recognition instead of moving toward self-actualization. Our educational system, the pressures of our careers, societal norms, and a lack of self-awareness all contribute to fostering this tendency.

The journey toward self-actualization is deeply personal and varies for each individual, contingent upon their values, circumstances, and the extent of their self-awareness.

Without an understanding of passion and purpose, individuals may find themselves aimlessly driving, stopping at every intersection, and feeling lost and frustrated. Having clarity is like pursuing a cause and actively striving to reach it, doing what you love doing. While this path may not guarantee an effortless passage, the challenges encountered along the way will be significant, worth it, and meaningful.

A significant portion of us are trapped in a monotonous routine. It starts with waking up in the morning, getting ready for work, spending our days in the office, attending long meetings and discussions that quite often yield no tangible outcomes. So, immersed in this routine, we forget that it doesn't align with our true desires or the life we envisioned, if we ever did envision it. Consequently, we find ourselves feeling trapped in a life that doesn't align with our dreams and aspirations. We fantasize about a dream job or a dream life, but no matter what we do, we remain trapped.

Often, our focus is directed towards what we "must do" rather than what we truly "wish to do."

This reminds me of the movie "The Secret Life of Walter Mitty," where the protagonist, played by Ben Stiller, leads a monotonous life within the confines of a mundane existence. Working for the same company for years, he's respected and competent at his job but trapped in a loop, repeating the same routine day after day. However, through unexpected events and adventures, he explores his true self and experiences a life-changing transformation.

Similarly, the Bollywood movie "Tamasha" is a thought-provoking film that explores the themes of self-discovery, passion, and the significance of living an authentic life in service of a cause. The protagonist, played by Ranbir Kapoor, leads a monotonous and scripted existence, conforming to societal expectations and suppressing his true self.

He adopts different personas to fit into societal roles and expectations of being a good child, following what is expected of him and others like him. He follows the predetermined path of education, career, and relationships, all while suppressing his true self, which is creative and spontaneous. He feels trapped and unfulfilled, yearning for a life that allows him to express his true essence.

As the story unfolds, the character faces challenges and setbacks, but he perseveres in his journey of self-discovery. He recognizes that conformity and societal expectations have hindered his personal growth and happiness. He realizes that he must break free from the confines of a scripted life and embrace his passions, even if it means facing uncertainties and societal disapproval. His true purpose, as it comes out, is to entertain people by expressing his creative thoughts, which reflects through his passion for storytelling and performing arts. By discovering his purpose and embracing his passion, he finds the motivation and determination to take meaningful actions in pursuit of his dreams.

"Tamasha" highlights the significance of finding one's true passion and purpose, living authentically, and breaking away from the shackles of societal norms. It encourages individuals to question the roles they play in society and to explore their unique talents and aspirations. It serves as a reminder that true fulfillment and happiness can only be achieved by embracing one's authentic self and pursuing one's passions, even if it means going against the usual.

This story is not so different from our own lives, for many. We often fail to explore our true potential and limit ourselves within the confines of our comfort zones. Our priorities change over time, and we convince ourselves that we're pursuing what we want. Yet, even after achieving those goals, we find ourselves back where we started. When it comes to envisioning our future and exploring our real selves, we seldom invest sufficient time and energy into it. We exhaust ourselves by devoting our time and energy to fulfilling someone else's purpose, goals, and expectations, losing sight of our own.

Whose vision are you fulfilling if not yours?

Strange as it may sound, you are working for the vision of others and not having any clarity of your own. Imagine working for a renowned multinational technology company that was founded decades ago by a visionary entrepreneur. The company has a grand vision of transforming the world through innovation and technological advancements. As an employee, you find yourself dedicated to fulfilling that vision, working tirelessly day after day, striving to meet the company's vision and goals.

However, amidst the hustle and bustle of corporate life, some of us realize that we have lost sight of our own vision or perhaps never took the time to figure it out. We become so engrossed in serving another's vision, whether or not it aligns with our own, that we overlook our individual path and fail to clarify what truly motivates us.

It's as if we're mere cogs in a wheel, contributing to a collective objective without a clear understanding of our personal vision. This is quite common in the fast-paced corporate life, where employees are caught up in the race of fulfilling companies' goals and vision, leaving no time for them to reflect on their own.

There's a company's vision, but does yours align with that? There are multiple possibilities, and most of them would require you to reassess your alignment.

Gaining clarity about our passion and purpose can bring a new sense of meaning and direction to our lives. This self-awareness is crucial, as it empowers us to make informed decisions about our lives. This includes gaining clarity not only on who we are and what we want to be but also recognizing our strengths, capabilities, and alignment with our aspirations.

Without awareness of these dimensions, many of us struggle to define the right path for ourselves, making random decisions that may ultimately prove unsatisfying. Many of us become entangled in so many pursuits that we lose sight of our true aspirations. This struggle is common, and it's okay to feel confused. What's important is acknowledging the lack of clarity and taking steps to address it.

My purpose is to support bringing transformative change in individuals by unlocking their true potential, enabling them to become the best version of themselves. I aim to achieve this through my passion for sharing knowledge.

This purpose (my "why" - supporting transformative change in individuals by unlocking their potential, enabling them to become the best version of themselves) gets fulfilled through what I am passionate about (my "how" - sharing knowledge through options like training, coaching, mentoring) and further shapes my action.

And what about you? If you're grappling with uncertainty about your passion and purpose, rest assured that you're not alone. Options exist (we will get to that in some time).

Gaining clarity allows us to set meaningful goals and make decisions that are in alignment with our values and aspirations. It helps us stay motivated and resilient, even in the face of challenges and obstacles. With a clear understanding of what we are passionate about and why it matters to us, one can chart a course for success and take intentional steps that lead us closer to our goals.

Synergy between purpose and passion is crucial for achieving success and fulfillment. When we have a strong sense of purpose and are deeply passionate about what we do, our actions become driven by a deep-rooted intrinsic motivation. We become more resilient, resourceful, and proactive in the pursuit of our goals. We are willing to invest the necessary time, effort, and sacrifices because we believe in the importance of our actions.

Meet Sarah. Eager to achieve independence, she entered the workforce after completing her graduation, echoing the path of many friends and classmates. While on the job, she pursued an MBA, inspired by her seniors and colleagues. She has been working as an office administrator for almost a decade now. Though she finds some satisfaction in her job, a sense of incompleteness nags at her. She goes through the motions, completing her tasks diligently, but deep down, she lacks a clear sense of purpose.

Sarah's daily routine consists of waking up, getting ready for work, commuting, spending long hours at the office, and returning home exhausted. On weekends, she tries to relax and catch up on personal errands, but she often feels unfulfilled and dreads the coming Monday.

She has never really taken the time to reflect on her true self. She hasn't explored her personal interests or pursued any hobbies outside of work. "Where's the time" is her constant excuse to herself and others. However, she did get inspired by many. Summing up her story, she finds herself in a constant state of stagnation, lacking direction and meaning, feeling envious and dissatisfied.

To highlight, she did indeed draw inspiration from various sources, venturing into different endeavors—some thrilling at the start, others mundane.

A lot of us navigate through our life without gaining clarity about our passion and purpose. The unfortunate fact is that we go through our daily routines, yet we don't take out the time to explore ourselves, engage in self-reflection, and take steps to gain that clarity.

"It's never too late until it's too late."

The opportunity for change persists as long as it hasn't elapsed into irrelevance. Discovering and pursuing a purpose that imbues life with meaning and satisfaction, doing what one loves doing, remains attainable at any point and any stage of life.

An Astounding Reality

We may be lagging in our understanding of ourselves, but with the technological advances, I think there will be a time when these systems would know more about us and our behavior than we do. That technology has started understanding us and suggesting what we need. I am amazed by the latest advancements in technology.

In today's digital era, we are consistently immersed in a landscape shaped by data and algorithms. These intricate systems capture our preferences, habits, and interests. Our online engagements, social media interactions, and browsing history leave behind a trail of information that is meticulously analyzed by technology platforms. For example, when you have a problem and you're trying to find a solution, technology starts providing you with solutions every day you interact with it (such as Google search and how you receive suggestions everywhere, including Facebook, Instagram, websites, etc.).

It's amazing and at the same time, it's scary. So far, it is limited to what we need to see and purchase; who knows what's in store for the future.

Ironically, while technology gathers vast amounts of data about us, many individuals struggle to have a clear understanding of themselves. They may feel lost, uncertain about their purpose, and unaware of their true desires. The constant bombardment of external influences, societal expectations, and the allure of materialistic pursuits often clouds their self-perception.

While technology may provide some glimpses into our preferences and behaviors, it is our own journey of self-discovery that holds the key to understanding ourselves fully. By actively seeking clarity and embracing self-awareness, we can have authority over our lives and navigate them with purpose, leading to a more fulfilling and authentic existence.

Follow your Passion

From childhood, the following suggestion has echoed persistently: "Follow your passion, and you will forever be happy, and success will follow you."

It sounded like a wonderful philosophy for living a fulfilling life. In fact, it seemed like convenient advice coming from people who themselves might be grappling with their own decisions or may never have explored any other options, believing this to be their best choice.

Meet Aman, who is in a lucrative corporate job and he is going places. From the outside, it may seem like he is successful, which he is – plush office, impressive title, and substantial income. However, he has that nagging feeling that something is missing.

Driven by the desire to find his passion and fulfillment, he began looking for options by speaking with his friends and colleagues who chose different paths for themselves. One of them was into traveling and blogging about various cultures, food, people, and was pretty successful. She had left her job a couple of years back, and Aman was one of the people who advised her against taking that decision.

Now inspired by her success and his liking for travel, he considered following similar footsteps, thinking that is the missing puzzle piece that's keeping him away from fulfillment. He took a sabbatical of 6 months and started on that path.

While his endeavor was enjoyable, it was just limited to a spark of inspiration, and it never did ignite a relentless pursuit.

Apparently, he liked the idea of traveling to places but lacked the patience that is required to plan, book accommodations, arrange itineraries, research etc. Addressing unforeseen challenges posed a stark contrast to his impulsive nature. The journey of following your passion entails one to embrace all experiences associated with a pursuit.

While "follow your passion" is good advice to give, it underscores the importance of differentiating between inspiration and true passion.

If I were to tell you "Follow your passion," what would you do? You would most likely start searching for it like you have always done, and perhaps after searching for it for some time, you would give up and continue on the path that you have. Or, like many, you would get inspired and consider that as your passion.

Let's try to understand first what does it mean to "follow your passion."

Passion:

Passion is a strong liking, desire, or deep interest in some activity. It's something that you are naturally inclined to do well, and to excel at it, you will continuously try to learn more about it by investing time and energy. It is intense, deep-rooted enthusiasm for something that you relentlessly pursue, fueled by love and dedication for that something.

It's there within you and is an integral part of your identity, however, most of the time you are searching for it externally.

Have you ever observed yourself? You are usually into many things—some experimenting, some just for fun, some casual, and certain things you do with utmost dedication, focus, and commitment. Where do you think you get that motivation to complete them without the thought of quitting?

When you are extremely passionate about something, it becomes a compelling reason for you to invest time and energy in continuously learning and growing. It comes from within and gives you a sense of achievement.

During my time in the corporate world, I used to mentor and coach individuals on process improvement. However, there's a crucial aspect that many people fail to understand. When I say I mentored and coached, I didn't mean that I would provide them with solutions on how to improve processes. Instead, I guided them to find their own solutions. I'll circle back to this point later.

Returning to my initial point, as I was approachable on a personal front, many sought advice beyond process enhancement and projects, seeking guidance on how to transition from their current roles as they had become mundane and monotonous, lacking challenges. They would ask, "How can I do what you're doing? What I am currently doing no longer excites me."

I was into process improvement, training, consulting, project mentoring, and coaching. To an outsider, all of these are apparently considered career boosters, and indeed they are, provided you approach them correctly and gain the right skills and experience, which takes time.

It's not their fault. Jobs can become monotonous over time when you find yourself repeating the same work again and again. Over time, the enthusiasm fades, work becomes boring, and you feel restricted, unable to explore beyond your current line of work.

In my own career journey, I started in operations, moved into business analytics, and eventually transitioned to quality. Within quality, where I spent about 60% of my collective work experience, I was fortunate to work with different sectors, making it a learning experience. During many discussions and trainings, I would share how my career evolved over the years, and people would express their desires to emulate my journey. However, when I asked them, "What do they really want to do or what excites them?" the usual response was silence or a vague statement like, "I admire what you're doing, and I want to follow a similar path."

What good would it be if after some time you realize that this is not for you and you have to start over or maybe fall back on what you were doing?

That's Inspiration, not Passion:

They come across as if they feel passionate about doing what I was doing, but more likely, they're inspired due to an appealing job profile. It's like defining a path without knowing the objective, rather having it otherwise.

This is a common mistake that a lot of us make. We get inspired by things for many reasons like a lack of challenges in our existing work, a lack of support, seeking quick growth opportunities, or a shortcut to success which, as I mentioned earlier, often comes down to more money, status, and other possessions. And we start assuming that the other person's path would fit into ours.

How is that different from what we have been doing all this while, which is following others' paths and being conformists? Think about it, how did you end up in your current career option? If it was by inspiration and it didn't work out in the past, what assurance does it hold for the future?

Most likely, the person's path that you intend to follow might himself be following someone else's path.

We get inspired by a lot of things, and most likely it won't last for long.

You may draw inspiration from someone who is passionate about their path, but in a world where nine out of ten individuals tread predefined trails without a clear understanding of why, it's easy to lose oneself in the crowd.

How did I get into being a quality guy? Well, it was a mix of inspiration and figuring out what I was passionate about, back in the year 2006. I had never considered becoming a part of this domain until one day I realized I had a knack for it. I was part of operations, and I got into doing some research. Soon, I had a revelation while doing that research. I started looking for more opportunities like that, and that's when I realized I had an affinity for this kind of work. So, as soon as I got the chance, I went to my bosses expressing my desire to do similar work. Since there was nothing available in that space, and I was after their life, they transferred me to business analytics. I had no idea what it was, and I had to do a process transition from the US. I learned the process and learned it well, was recognized, rewarded, and awarded during the transition and got promoted afterward. Subsequently, I moved into the quality space, did more transitions, and received more recognition. If you have seen the movie "A Beautiful Mind," Russell Crowe is a code breaker, and when he sees numbers, he visualizes a pattern. However funny it may sound, but I can associate with that as I always believed each number/data point is part of a big story. As you start connecting those points, the real story emerges, like if you remember, we used to play a game wherein you connect the dots, and an image gets revealed. Even though the journey that I just mentioned sounds easy through and through, it was not.

Passion will drive you to keep moving forward despite the challenges. If you fail, you will try again with a different strategy, and all along, your motivation to move forward will remain high. In the past couple of years, I have not been successful in many pursuits, but every morning I am back at it with the same enthusiasm and motivation.

This does not mean that you will be passionate about one thing and one thing only, but as you mature with age, knowledge, and wisdom, passion evolves in tandem. I still enjoy data crunching, but I have also grown to appreciate other pursuits like coaching and training. Even though a part of my work remains in the same field, my passion evolves while the underlying patterns of interest remain. I have always had an analytical mind, and I still do. I was curious about things, and I still ask a lot of questions, sometimes enough to annoy others.

Throughout my journey, I have pursued various other interests. Adventure-seeking, observing and assimilating new experiences, sharing knowledge, ideation, and challenging the status quo have consistently remained part of my ventures, regardless of the specific pursuit.

When you are inspired and follow someone's path, at some point, when you face obstacles, you may start looking for new inspiration and another path to follow.

Don't be trapped by inspiration, find your path

Sometime back, someone approached me. This individual was feeling stuck in what she was doing, and by the way she was doing okay. During our conversation, while trying to explore different avenues, she got inspired, prompting her to consider the same path as mine. The grass does look greener on the other side, but remember it's not a linear path. I have no issues if someone gets inspired and follows similar path but when there will be obstacles, and there will be revelations about the choices. What then? Will you keep pushing yourself to do what isn't you?

The immense potential within each one of us remains wasted because we get inspired by other people's lifestyles, work, etc., and we assume that is the one for us. We fail to explore what aligns with our true selves and follow what we assume is the one.

People often confuse inspiration with passion, blurring the distinction between the two. It is common for individuals to feel inspired by something and mistake that feeling as a sign of their passion. However, there are important distinctions between the two.

It's possible to be inspired by something without it being true passion. People get inspired by many things, and that does not necessarily mean they are passionate about it.

Simran got inspired by a successful friend entrepreneur and felt motivated to start her own business. However, as she delves deeper into the challenges and realities of entrepreneurship, she realized that her initial inspiration was not aligned with her true passion. She discovered that her passion lies in a different field altogether.

Passion vs. Inspiration

It's important to understand the distinction between passion and inspiration for personal growth and fulfillment.

Inspiration is a surge of motivation from others, a spark that ignites the imagination. It is a momentary burst of motivation that comes from external sources such as observing someone's work, listening to an inspiring story, or getting an idea. This inspiration ignites a strong desire to pursue a goal or endeavor.

Embarking on the path of self-discovery requires us to re-evaluate our choices, passions, and desires. It's about acknowledging that our initial choices might not have been aligned with our true selves and seeking opportunities that resonate deeply.

Sarah, the office administrator we mentioned earlier, took a moment to pause and reflect on her daily routine. By delving into her experiences, she might realize that her true passion lies in community engagement and helping others. With this newfound insight, she could explore roles that allow her to make a meaningful impact and contribute to causes she truly cares about. These roles don't necessarily require her to quit her current one. She began building on it within her current role, for instance, she started volunteering in CSR activities within the organization to begin with. Eventually, after some time, she transitioned into a full-time role pursuing her passion and a cause she truly felt passionate about. This shift from merely fulfilling a job description to pursuing a purpose-driven role/career transformed her outlook on work and life.

In the past, I was inspired by writers and thought about writing, but that didn't mean I started writing. Remember, it evolves, and I began writing a little bit here and there, and then this book happened much later.

Do passionate people quit? "No," because they are constantly learning, challenging the status quo, and outgrowing their capabilities to reach the next level of potential.

Your passion fuels actions, determination, resilience, unwavering dedication, and commitment to pursue and persist even in the face of challenges.

On the other hand, people experiencing a surge of motivation and enthusiasm may be prompted to take action. However, inspiration alone does not provide the same level of motivation and commitment when faced with challenges. They may lose interest later.

A passionate artist spends years honing their craft, constantly pushing their creative boundaries and striving for excellence. They face rejection and criticism, but their deep love for art keeps them going. Even during times of self-doubt or financial struggles, they persist because their passion is what drives them. On the other hand, an inspired artist may embark on a creative project after being inspired by someone else's work, but when faced with challenges or a lack of immediate success, they may lose interest and abandon the project.

I'm sure you've heard this thousands of times: "You need to feel passionate about what you do." When you hear this, you might start searching for your passion in what you are currently doing or in something else. How about gaining clarity on the same and incorporating that into your life?

It takes a lot of effort to truly find your passion, and many spend their lives without ever discovering their authentic calling because they may not be looking in the right place, fear failure, lack patience, or give up too early. Some jump from one endeavor to another, hoping to find their calling. However, their focus is frequently misdirected, resulting in brief enthusiasm followed by a return to stagnation. They get into doing stuff, and after some time, they struggle to find that feeling.

I was in a corporate setup for 20 years. It was a good run for the most part, and then it started going downhill sometime around 2016/17. I was good at my job and I liked it, but I didn't love it, and this was not how I envisioned my future. It stopped being challenging. Something inside of me kept me restless. I knew there was more to life than this.

There is a distinction between liking something and loving it. You may like something because it serves a purpose, but that may not necessarily be your life's purpose.

So, when it started going downhill, all I was doing was following a routine until a point when I was literally dragging myself to the office, working from 9 to 5, completing the tasks I had to do, and adding no value to the job or myself.

Honestly, I had never imagined myself in a desk job, but I ended up in one eventually just because I never explored to gain clarity on what I truly desired. So, I followed the most usual and common path.

It's a lot easier and more comfortable than spending time and energy seeking clarity and taking actions on that. So, I did what most others do: find a job and then hop from one to another looking for growth, money, status, etc.

Money was good, companies were good, the annual increments and bonuses were also good, and it all helped me provide more than a decent living for myself and my family. All was good, but it lacked fulfillment and happiness, with a constant reminder that there is more to this.

So, I was stuck:

- Lacking energy and excitement in what I did, living life on autopilot following the same routine day in and day out.
- Feeling disengaged and dispassionate about work and people.
- Lacking inspiration to go beyond the assigned tasks.
- Not feeling like contributing more.
- Constantly questioning my purpose (why am I doing what I am doing).
- Not finding it challenging enough or not feeling like taking on new challenges.
- Experiencing flattened learning.
- Having no clear goals, feeling like it's a drag.
- Anxiously waiting for weekends.
- Being risk-averse or avoiding risks.
- Engaging in non-productive tasks.
- Viewing the job as just a routine.

"Fulfillment is when your passion serves a purpose."

The journey involves discovering a passion that serves your purpose. It lies within each one of us. You can either find it yourself or seek help from someone, but I urge you not to emulate others because if you do, it may lead you right back into this struggle sooner or later, and who knows what the situation will be then.

Change now if you feel the need for it, rather than waiting until you believe you're fully prepared for it. The truth is, you'll never feel completely ready. We often wait for situations to get better before taking a chance, but it's always "tomorrow," and we all know tomorrow never comes.

"We wait for the circumstances to change, knowing very well that it is the circumstances that we want to change." - Viktor Frankl

You can't create passion; you can only experience it.

Fascinatingly, you regularly, or perhaps even on a daily basis, encounter moments and engage in activities that elicit varying levels of energy, enthusiasm, and engagement. You might not have realized it, but perhaps this is the signal you should pay attention to when searching for your true passion.

For instance, in the morning, you may start your day by exercising, and you find that it captivates your interest and energizes your mind. You become completely absorbed, experiencing a high level of engagement and a surge of energy. This suggests that physical activity is something that captivates your interest and energizes you, indicating it might be a potential area of interest for you.

During the same day, while attending a team meeting at work, you notice that your energy level fluctuates. At times, when the topic aligns with your expertise or sparks your interest, you are willing to invest time and energy to learn and contribute more. You feel highly engaged and enthusiastic, radiating positive energy. However, during other parts of the meeting that may not directly pertain to your role or interests, your engagement level dips, and your energy diminishes slightly.

In the evening, you immerse yourself in the creative process, and time seems to fade away. You don't realize that you have spent hours until someone tells you or you check the time. Your energy levels soar, and you are completely absorbed in the act of painting, experiencing a deep sense of fulfillment and a heightened state of focus and joy.

It's important to note that while sensing energy, enthusiasm, or high engagement during specific activities—like the morning exercise or discussions about your favorite topics—can provide insights, true passion reveals itself through recurring patterns. Rather than defining your passion solely based on these moments, seek out consistent trends.

Understanding these fluctuations empowers you to identify tasks that engage you and activities that sap your energy. It's all about designing your life, making choices that align with your desires and strengths.

In the words of Professor Mihaly Csikszentmihalyi, what you just experienced is a state of FLOW. There are 8 characteristics of FLOW, and they are:

- Complete concentration on the task.
- Clarity of goals and immediate feedback.
- Transformation of time (speeding up or slowing down).
- Intrinsic reward and fulfillment.
- Effortlessness and ease.
- Balance between challenge and skills.
- Merging of actions and awareness, losing self-consciousness.
- A sense of control over the task.

According to him, when your skills align with the challenge at hand, you are in a state of Flow. Conversely, when your skills are lower than the challenge, you may feel anxious, and if your skills surpass the challenge, you will easily get bored. When that happens, you may be inclined to quit the task or do the task without full dedication.

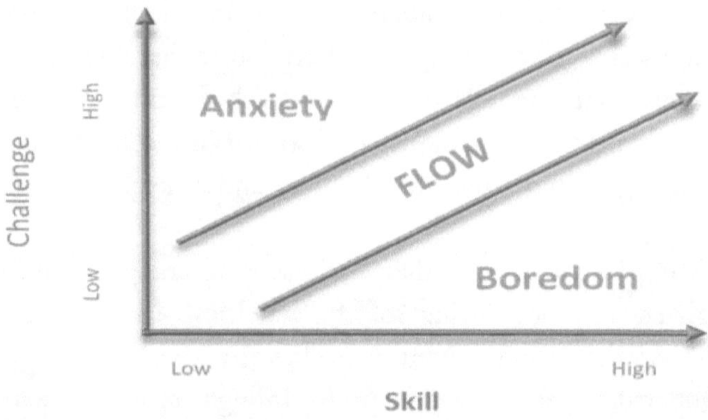

Have you ever encountered moments when you were so deeply engrossed in an activity that you lost track of time? You would spend hours on that task without feeling the need for breaks, totally engrossed in the activity despite distractions or interruptions. That was a flow moment for you.

When we talk about engagement, we're trying to identify low-engagement tasks, activities, or moments when you feel bored, dull, unhappy, restless, or even anxious. On the other hand, high engagement refers to when you are happy, excited while doing something, focused, and genuinely enjoy the activity.

When it comes to energy, many times you start a task with high energy, but as time passes, you lose that energy, and by the end of it, you are totally exhausted. Then there are activities that might tire you physically, but your energy levels remain higher. For example, on any normal day, you may go to the office with high energy, but a few tasks later, your energy is drained because of a meeting or a discussion with your boss. At that point, you wish the day would end, and nothing seems exciting thereafter.

Similarly, if the first few tasks are something you enjoy doing, your energy remains high despite being physically tired, and you are ready to face more challenges for the rest of the day.

Many times, we form conclusions about something without a good understanding of it. You may hate your job, role, organization, colleagues, or relations, but when you break down the moments into chunks, within those chunks, there are moments you hate and moments where you were high on energy, very engaged, probably in a state of flow.

You need to understand what works for you and what doesn't. Understand those moments and activities that you like, which you wouldn't have realized in the normal course because you disliked the overall experience.

While working in a corporate role, I realized that I loved giving trainings and conducting workshops, process and project management, and analyzing data. I also enjoyed problem-solving, brainstorming and ideation sessions. What I disliked was lengthy unproductive meetings, chase people for tasks and updates, unable to influence or guide important decisions, creating and updating presentations for unnecessary meetings and discussions, and most importantly, not being acknowledged for the work done. Understanding this aspect of your life creates choices for you, and that's part of designing your life.

When looking for a job or making career choices, you might have often chosen from what was available or what the role required, even if it wasn't explained well to you and involved tasks you didn't enjoy. This could be due to a lack of choices or a lack of clarity.

However, now you realize the importance of understanding this aspect of your life. By gaining a deeper understanding of your desires, strengths, and values, you open up a world of possibilities and create choices for yourself. Instead of hastily accepting the first option that presents itself, you embrace the idea of designing your life.

For instance, let's say you have a passion for writing and storytelling. In the past, you may have taken any job that seemed remotely related to writing or maybe a totally different one, simply because it seemed like a good opportunity that came your way. But now, with a clearer understanding, you explore various paths that align with your passion. You have a choice to consider options such as becoming a novelist, a journalist, or a content creator. However, it's important to note that taking up such choices does not necessarily mean that quitting the job is the only option. You could do freelance work alongside your job or explore other options.

Being passionate about something doesn't mean that you have all the relevant skills to make it big. You may be a beginner who has a long way to go, with many things to learn, and quitting may not be the right option at this time (we will talk about this in a little while).

By consciously designing your life and seeking out choices that resonate with your true desires, you embark on a journey of self-discovery and fulfillment. You no longer settle for convenience or uncertainty. Instead, you embrace the power of choice and create a life that aligns with your authentic self.

Flow Exploration

Objective: Explore your passion and discover activities that bring you into a state of flow.

Instructions:
- Allocate a specific time each day or week for this exploration. Treat it as a delightful adventure of self-discovery.
- Create a Flow Exploration Journal where you will document your reflections and observations.
- Recall activities/past experiences: Take a moment to reflect on your past experiences where you felt completely absorbed and in the state of flow. It could be any activity, project, hobby, or even a moment in your personal or professional life. Try to vividly remember the details of those experiences.
- For each flow experience, recollect the details and write down the following information:
  - Activity: Describe the specific activity you were immersed in during that experience, breaking it into components (chunks). For instance, if you were working on a software

development project, you'd mention tasks like requirements analysis, coding, testing, debugging, documentation, and release. You can further break down tasks to more granular chunks to better understand your engagement levels and preferences within a broader activity. You might find that your engagement is at its peak during the coding and debugging phases, but it tends to dip when you're documenting the code.

- Location: Note the physical or virtual location where the activity took place.
- Interaction: Identify the people involved in the activity, such as colleagues, friends, or family members.

- Reflect on the qualities: Once you have a specific experience in mind, reflect on the qualities and characteristics of that flow state. Ask yourself the following questions and write down your answers:
  - What were you doing during that experience?
  - What skills or abilities were you utilizing?
  - Were there any challenges or obstacles you overcame?
  - How did you feel mentally, emotionally, and physically during that experience?
  - Did time seem to fly by, and were you completely immersed in the present moment?
  - Identify common elements: Look for common repeatable patterns and elements among these flow experiences. Write down the common elements and take note of them. Consider the following aspects:
  - Skills and abilities: Were there specific skills or abilities that you utilized during these experiences (e.g., physical, intellectual, creative, social)?
  - Challenge level: What was the level of challenge you faced during those activities? Was it low, medium, or high? Did it push you out of your comfort zone?

- Interest: Reflect on the level of interest you had while doing those activities. Were you motivated to engage in those tasks?
- Goals: Were you clear about the goals to be achieved? Did you have a sense of progress, instant feedback, and a feeling of accomplishment as you moved through accomplishing milestones?
- Immersion and time distortion: Did you lose track of time and become fully immersed in the activity? Were you able to maintain focus despite external distractions?
- Enjoyment: Did you enjoy being fully immersed in the activity? Did it bring a sense of satisfaction and joy?

- Analyze patterns: Take a moment to reflect on common repeatable patterns and elements, their significance, and how they relate to your personal values and interests. Understanding this connection will guide you in seeking out similar activities or creating opportunities that incorporate these elements.
- Consider personal values and interests: Reflect on whether these flow experiences align with your personal values and interests. Do they reflect your passions or talents? Consider how these flow-inducing activities can be incorporated into your life.
  - Personal values: Think about the values that are important to you. Are the activities that trigger your flow state in alignment with those values? For example, if creativity is a core value for you, consider if your flow experiences involve creative pursuits.
  - Interests and passions: Examine whether your flow experiences reflect your interests and passions. What tasks, subjects, or hobbies ignite your curiosity and enthusiasm? Identifying these interests will help you recognize activities that align with your passions.
  - Talents and strengths: Reflect on the skills, abilities, or talents you possess that contribute to your flow experiences. Are there specific areas where you excel and feel a sense

of fulfillment? Recognizing your strengths can guide you towards activities that leverage those talents.

- Set intentions: Based on your reflections, set intentions for incorporating more flow-inducing activities into your life. Consider how you can create opportunities to engage in activities that align with your flow triggers and bring you joy.

- Experiment and explore: Don't be afraid to explore new activities and try different approaches. The flow state can be found in various domains, so be open to discovering new interests and passions.

- Create a Passion Map that outlines the activities, skills, challenges, interests, goals, situations, behavior, people, time, location, and other common elements that trigger your flow state. This map will serve as a guide to help you seek out similar activities and incorporate more flow-inducing experiences into your life, aligned with your personal values and interests. Remember to be open-minded and willing to explore new opportunities along your journey of discovering and nurturing your passions. Rate the elements that stand out to you on this map.

Based on my personal exploration and recognizing a recurring pattern, it became clear that the values and skills I closely associated with were creativity, analytical thinking, and problem-solving. The tasks that invoked these interests were when I was engaged in sharing knowledge, data analytics, and actively contributing to individual or process improvement. On the flip side, I had a dislike for administrative tasks.

Applying this insight, I honed in on my passion for training and workshops, coaching, and consulting. I became a trainer, offering workshops on topics such as leadership development, communication skills, or continuous improvement. Additionally, I started working as a coach for individuals and a consultant for organizations, helping them in their continuous improvement efforts. This allowed me to have greater control over the tasks, including the ability to outsource or delegate certain activities.

Need

Now, let's talk about the need. Once you've identified what comes naturally to you or what you love doing, the key lies in considering how to leverage this information. This self-awareness is invaluable and offers you choice. You can either leave it at the level of awareness or take it a step further by integrating the Flow patterns you've recognized into your daily, or if not daily, then regular life. If your aim involves a career transformation, this self-awareness can serve as a compass to explore opportunities that align with your natural inclinations.

Imagine getting paid for what you genuinely love doing – that's the pinnacle of a fulfilling career. For that to happen, you need to understand whether there's a need in the world out there for what you love doing. Striking a balance between both may require some creativity, adaptability, and strategic thinking. This should enable you to embark on a journey to integrate your passion into your daily life and potentially transform it into a fulfilling career.

This may involve researching emerging trends, networking with professionals in related fields, or seeking mentorship and guidance from experts who have successfully integrated their passion into their careers. Through this process, you can discover innovative ways to apply your passion, create value for others, and find avenues where your skills and enthusiasm are sought after.

Alignment Between Passion and Market Need:

Objective: Analyzing the alignment between what you love doing (Passion) and the existing market need to identify potential opportunities for integration.

Instructions:

Prepare a Four-Blocker Grid: Create a grid with four quadrants, labeling the Y-axis as "Passion" (ranging from Low to High) and the X-axis as "Need" (ranging from Low to High). This will result in four quadrants: Low Passion/Low Need, Low Passion/High Need, High Passion/Low Need, and High Passion/High Need.

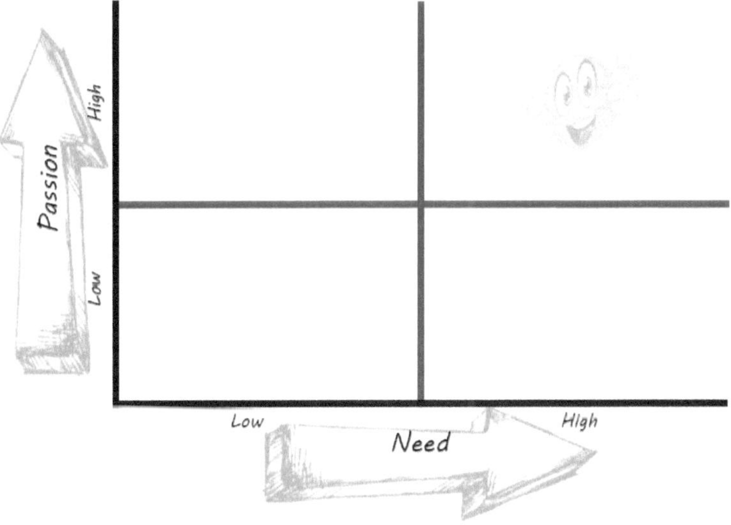

- Research market need:
  - Gain a deep understanding if there is a need for what you're passionate about.
  - Explore who would benefit from it, the challenges they encounter, and how you can address those challenges.
- Assess the potential impact of your work and whether people would be willing to pay for it.

- Collect data:
  - Gather relevant information from reports, publications, or online sources related to your area of interest.
  - Consider conducting online surveys to gather opinions and insights on the needs, challenges, and preferences of your target audience.
  - Reach out to your desired audience through social media and professional networks to gather feedback.
- Analyze the data:
  - Identify common themes and patterns or recurring needs that indicate a strong alignment between your passion and market need. Use the Four-Blocker grid to categorize the alignment.
  - Focus on areas of opportunities where your passion aligns with the market need, especially those in the top right quadrant of the grid (High Love doing and High Need).
- Reflect and strategize:
  - Reflect on how well your passion aligns with the identified market need and the potential impact you could have.
  - Develop plans and strategies to integrate your passion into addressing the market need. Set goals, define timelines, and outline the resources required to pursue the identified opportunities.

Remember, the ultimate goal is to find a quadrant in the top right of the Four-Blocker that represents a strong alignment between your passion and the need. This alignment signifies a potential path to pursue that can provide both personal fulfillment and meet the needs of others.

The same exercise can be applied to other aspects of life as well. For instance, if you are using this approach to improve your relationship with your partner, instead of comparing what you "Love doing" with the "Need," you could compare it to the "Joy" it brings into the relationship.

It's important to note that what you're searching for may not necessarily be entirely different from your current path. Your current path may already fulfill all the above criteria, but there might be less engaging tasks that cast a shadow over the aspects you truly enjoy.

Passion without need is a hobby.

For example, someone might have an intense passion for collecting stamps. They may spend countless hours researching, organizing, and learning about different stamps. However, stamp collecting is a niche interest that doesn't have broad commercial appeal. Therefore, it remains a hobby rather than a viable career path.

Skill

Now, consider the role of skill. Imagine you are deeply passionate about sustainable living and eco-friendly practices. As you explore this passion, you notice a rising trend in the market for eco-conscious products and services. People are becoming more environmentally conscious and actively seeking solutions that have a reduced negative impact on the planet. This presents a golden opportunity for you to contribute positively while making a difference.

So, can you bridge the gap between your passion, the market need, and your contribution? The key often lies in your skillset. Your skills can enable you to effectively translate your passion into a meaningful contribution that meets the needs of the market.

The ability to bridge the gap between your passion, market need, and contribution often lies in your skillset. Consider the following scenario: You've been working at a multinational call center for 5 years, and you've had intentions of joining an organization that specializes in sustainable solutions at some point. However, life happened, and you got busy, feeling trapped due to the misalignment between your true passion and your current reality. You want to make your passion a reality, but making the leap requires more than just good intentions.

Why should an organization hire you for something you are passionate about but lack the skills for? While you may have engaged in corporate social responsibility (CSR) activities promoting eco-friendly solutions, bought eco-friendly products during festive seasons, or even planted many trees around your house or campus, these efforts demonstrate genuine concern and initiative to contribute, but they might not be enough to transition into a new career.

The dilemma you face is that you can't entirely jump into your idea because you lack experience and skills. However, quitting the idea due to this lack of experience and skills will continue to make you feel trapped in your current reality, which provides you with money and luxuries but lacks satisfaction. You may switch organizations with similar work profiles, be excited for a while, but eventually find yourself back in the same routine.

If you aspire to elevate your passion from a mere concern level to a sustainable career option, possessing relevant skills is crucial. Remember that the concept of "Flow" is founded on a balance between skill and challenges. When challenges are greater than your skills, anxiety sets in, and if it's the other way around, boredom sets in. Neither of these options is conducive to a fulfilling journey. Therefore, acquiring the necessary skills is essential to make your passion a viable and satisfying career option.

Starting a new journey, or in this case, acquiring new skills, does not necessarily mean that what you have learned so far goes to waste. There are certain skills that may not be directly applicable but can still hold relevance in the new context. Skills like effective communication, problem-solving, project management, etc., can be leveraged to make the transition smoother. It's important to identify and recognize these transferable skills.

On the other hand, there are skills that you may need to acquire over time. The journey of acquiring new skills is an ongoing process. You may need to take courses, attend workshops, and engage in volunteering activities. Additionally, don't underestimate the importance of other sources such as coaches, mentors, networking events, communities, and conferences. Connecting with people who have established themselves in the area of your passion can provide valuable guidance, and being part of communities can be beneficial for building relationships and gaining knowledge.

Don't quit your current job immediately. Instead, start working on acquiring the skills and knowledge needed for your desired career path. Take small steps toward making your desired option a reality. The advantage of taking small steps is that it can serve as a pilot run, allowing you to gauge your interest, make improvements if necessary, before transitioning completely.

Acquiring skills takes time, which is why we are focusing on creating a blueprint of success in this book. This blueprint empowers you to lay the foundation for a journey that balances aspiration with preparation, ensuring a smoother transition toward your passion-driven career.

Skill Assessment and Upskilling Action Plan

Objective: Assess your current skill level and create an action plan to upskill yourself from a Beginner level to an Expert level, enabling you to effectively deliver on your identified passion and achieve your desired objectives.

Identify Needed Skills:
- Connect with people and communities to identify and list the specific skills required for your passion-based objectives.
- If necessary, break these skills down into smaller, more manageable pieces.
- Create a skill map or a mind map depicting all the skills required to pursue your passion.

- Check Your Skill Level:
  - Rate your proficiency in each skill area on a scale from Beginner to Expert.

- Be honest with yourself during this assessment.

- Identify Gaps:
  - Compare your current skill level with the desired level for each skill.
  - Identify the areas where there are skill gaps that need to be addressed.
  - Recognize skills that you already possess, which can add value to what you seek to accomplish in your passion-driven career.
- Prioritize and Plan:
  - Plan how you will acquire these skills, considering whether you can do it part-time or full-time.
  - Prioritize the skills that are critical and aligned with your specific objectives.
  - Identify Learning Sources: Explore various learning sources such as courses, books, mentors, workshops, and online resources.
  - Manage Learning: Define milestones and timelines for acquiring each skill. Break down the process into manageable steps to avoid feeling overwhelmed.
  - Identify Other Sources: Consider opportunities like volunteering, becoming an intern, or freelancing in your spare time to gain practical experience.
  - Get Support: Connect with people who can provide guidance, support, and encouragement as you work towards your skill development goals.
  - Track Progress: Keep a record of your progress in acquiring each skill. Don't forget to elaborate successful achievements of milestones to stay motivated. Be open to improvising and adapting your plan as required.

Passion for	Skills Required	Skill Level		Gaps	Action Plan	Timelines
		Current	Desired			
		Beginner, Average, Competent, Expert	Beginner, Average, Competent, Expert			

Follow the established schedule and engage in the identified learning activities to carry out your action plan. Maintain your commitment, dedication, and consistency in your efforts to acquire the necessary abilities.

Remember, upskilling is an ongoing process that involves commitment, perseverance, and a growth mindset. Reassess your skill levels on a regular basis, revise your action plan, and look for opportunities to practice and use your newly gained talents. By systematically upskilling yourself, you will improve your abilities and effectiveness in delivering on your identified passion, whether it is for a professional change or the transformation of other elements of your life.

Purpose

Purpose serves a cause greater than self and uncovers the answer to the fundamental question, "Why are you doing what you are doing?"

Purpose serves as the focal point of a life devoted to a cause greater than oneself, transcending personal needs. It's who you are rather than who you feel compelled to be, and it goes beyond your material needs. Our life, in real sense, is all about making an impact for others and, consequently, ourselves, although we frequently find ourselves focused solely on making ends meet. I bet there isn't a role or job that doesn't serve a purpose.

When I say a cause greater than self, I basically mean the one that resonates with you and not just any cause or rather inspired from others' cause. To find the one you associate with:

Reflect back on the "explore your passion" exercise. Consider how your skills, interests, and passions can be channeled toward making a positive impact. A cause that resonates with you and your Flow patterns, bringing you joy and having the potential to create a positive impact for others.

By associating your flow-inducing activities with a cause you deeply associate with, you can find a powerful sense of purpose in your pursuits. It transforms your passion into a force for good, allowing you to make a meaningful impact while experiencing personal fulfillment.

"Your happiness cannot be your purpose but your purpose can lead to your happiness"

Your "why" is a driving force that carries you forward in life. If whatever you do serves that purpose, you will experience fulfillment and happiness. Your "why" encompasses the very essence of your life's purpose. It is more than just a career choice; it's your calling that gives direction to your life. It defines who you are.

Without knowing your "why," your "how" and "what" become meaningless.

Mostly, we focus on the tangible outcome or the "what," often ignoring the "why" and the "how."

Your "what" (aspirational life): We often desire a happy life with money, luxuries, status, a leadership position, and a corner office in a multinational corporation, assuming that all these things will bring happiness. Remember, they can, but it's often temporary.

Your "how": Achieving those aspirations by following the conventional path of success.

Not having clarity about your "why" can be a significant challenge in life. Understanding your purpose and why you do what you do is essential. It should enrich the lives of others and, in turn, positively impact your own life by elevating your sense of fulfillment and satisfaction. When I say impact, I'm not referring to money or status.

Many individuals, including myself, have grappled with this question. It can take hours or even days of self-exploration to find clarity. Often, people confuse their "why" with the "what." They think that their best life or the life they envision is their "why." The twist is that it's their "what," the outcome or the aspirational reality. True clarity comes when they understand their "why" and the "how" necessary to achieve that outcome, guiding them toward their aspirational reality "what."

Here's an example illustrating the concepts of "why," "how," and "what":

What (Aspirational Life): My vision for an aspirational life is one filled with happiness and fulfillment. It involves living a life where I can make a significant impact on others, witnessing their growth and transformation as they tap into their immense capabilities. I envision a life where I continuously learn, grow, and contribute. Additionally, the envisioned life provides me with enough resources to support the life I wish to pursue and other interests.

Vision Board Canvas

Why (Purpose): My purpose in life is to "help individuals unleash their full potential, which remains largely untapped." I believe in a cause greater than myself, and I am driven to contribute to the growth and development of others.

How (Approach): Fill the gap between "why" and "what." I intend to achieve my purpose by designing a life that aligns with my passions and interests. I am deeply passionate about sharing knowledge, assisting others, and providing training and coaching. These are the avenues through which I can best serve and support individuals in reaching their fullest potential.

By understanding my "why" (purpose), developing the blueprint "how" (blueprint, the roadmap) that aligns with my passions, and striving for the envisioned "what" (aspirational life), I aim to lead a fulfilling and impactful existence dedicated to helping individuals become their best selves.

Looking at the picture above, I am sure you've had some laughs trying to figure out my "what." Well, there's no obligation to decipher it, and if you still want to, keep guessing. Actually, it's my "what" based on my perception of what will give me happiness and fulfillment. But let me still try to explain. Sunrise and a contented smile represent me being happy with my endeavors. Blooming flower and the butterfly signify growth and transformation in myself and others. Shaking hands (if that looks like a shaking hand) represents the intention to make a significant impact on others. Diverse faces represent diverse communities or groups of people getting impacted by what I do. And then there are activities that I would love to do or continue (paragliding, biking, scuba, and more).

This is my way of depicting; you will have your way. As long as you relate to the picture you have drawn and understand the components, it doesn't matter if others understand it or not. Remember, it's the journey of your transformation.

Purpose, a continuous personal journey

Discovering one's purpose is a deeply personal and introspective journey. It requires self-reflection, exploration, and an understanding of one's passion, values, and aspirations. It may take time and effort to gain clarity on one's purpose, but it can provide a sense of direction, motivation, and fulfillment in life.

Each individual's purpose is distinct, and it has the potential to evolve and change over time as life circumstances and priorities shift. It's important to embrace the journey of self-discovery and continuously reassess and align one's actions with their sense of purpose to lead a meaningful and fulfilling life.

Your Purpose Statement:

To uncover your purpose, it can be helpful to revisit the exercise of discovering your passions. Combine the elements of what you love doing, has a cause greater than self, and the existence of a genuine need in the world around, to craft your purpose statement. Create a purpose statement that articulates how you can make a positive impact in the world, based on what you love doing and recognition of a genuine need.

This purpose statement will serve as a guiding light, directing your actions and choices toward making a meaningful contribution to the world.

Remember, the journey of purpose discovery is ongoing, and it is essential to regularly evaluate and adjust your actions to ensure they align with your evolving understanding of your purpose. By doing so, you can lead a purposeful life that brings fulfillment not only to yourself but also to those around you.

Passion+ Cause + Need = Purpose Statement

Passion without purpose is action without direction. It's like wandering without a clear direction. It involves engaging in activities you love without any specific objectives to be achieved. While these activities may bring you happiness and excitement, they often lack a profound sense of fulfillment.

I am a paraglider pilot and indulge in this pursuit solely for adventure and excitement. While I could have pursued it professionally, I refrained. Upon introspection and life design, I realized that transforming my passion into a profession might have led to disillusionment and even unintentional harm. Recognizing that my passion for paragliding, while exhilarating, didn't serve a greater purpose, was enlightening.

Purpose without passion is a vision without the drive to pursue it. Having a purpose without genuine passion is similar to making goals without the motivation to follow through on them. While you may have a clear grasp of what needs to be done, the lack of genuine passion and enthusiasm can lead to procrastination and a slew of excuses, discouraging you from following your goals completely.

When you're genuinely passionate about something, your emotional investment and excitement create a powerful motivational force. Without passion, the objective might remain theoretical, lacking the emotional engagement required to initiate and sustain action.

Imagine my purpose (described earlier), and I am trying to fulfill that purpose using online mediums like podcasts, webcasts, blogs, and articles. Although I do enjoy these methods to some extent, they don't provide the same satisfaction as sharing knowledge through live human interactions. Maintaining consistency poses a challenge. By the way, I did try that, started writing articles, blogs, and even webcasts, but I realized I yearn for human interaction. You're more likely to procrastinate and eventually abandon the goal altogether.

Passion in actions and directed towards your purpose is being in Flow

The key to finding fulfillment and achieving success lies in the integration of passion and purpose. When you engage in activities you love and direct them toward a meaningful goal, you experience a state of "flow". And the satisfaction you will derive from that will be immense. This state of flow is characterized by deep engagement, enjoyment, and a sense of being in sync with your purpose. That's what we are aiming for.

Success and fulfilling happiness lie in living your purpose by doing what you love.

Tony Robbins once said, "If you change nothing, nothing will change," and change necessitates actions!

So right now, you have the opportunity to create an exciting future for yourself. Re-think and re-invent yourself.

Design your passion to serve your life's purpose

Passion is for self, and purpose is for others. Both are within us; however, if we search at all, we tend to search outwards instead of searching inwards. This can result in:

- Pursuing the wrong passion and purpose and working hard to get there, eventually realizing at some point that it was not the one.

- Believing that you lack both passion and purpose. That usually happens when you haven't explored yourself, and circumstances have led you to assume that what you're doing is your purpose and passion.

- Being afraid of venturing into new territory.

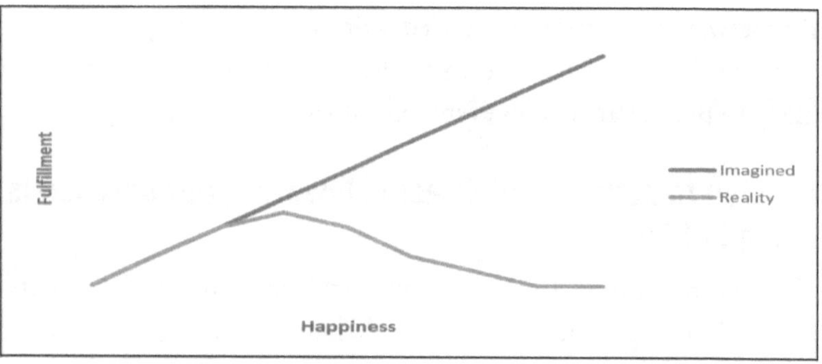

I've lived through these phases. Initially content, happiness dwindled. It's not that I was in a bad job; I was in a good one, and I liked doing what I did until it started going downhill. I was feeling stuck because it was not challenging anymore, and at a subconscious level, I could feel that it was not aligned. As I mentioned earlier, I lacked absolute clarity. While I used to do training and other things that I liked, but not often. Later, while exploring, I could see the peaks of energy, excitement, and enthusiasm during those times.

Eventually, it was just a job, a means to an end, lacking any new learning and personal growth. So instead of looking forward to getting back to the office every day, I was looking forward to the weekend and vacations.

Since 2019, post-corporate life, I have a different perspective, a much broader one, gained clarity of my purpose. Now I have designed my life to serve that purpose, which is:

"To help individuals and organizations be their best self by tapping into their immense and yet underutilized potential."

There's a lot of potential that lays wasted, and my purpose is to help individuals like myself gain clarity and live their purpose. What I did, and you can replicate too, is to "Design your passion to serve your life's purpose."

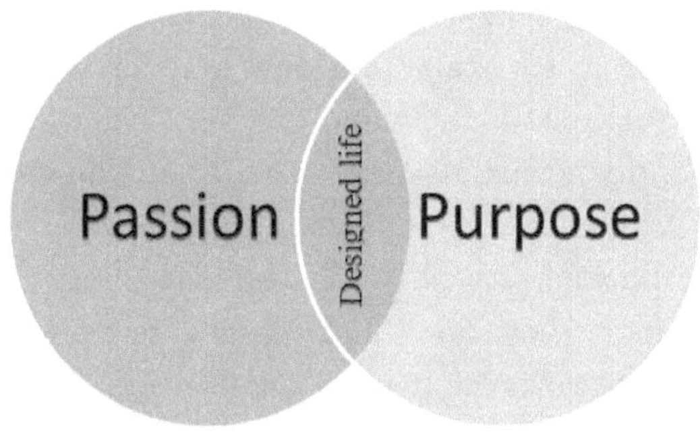

By understanding your purpose, nurturing your passions, and intentionally designing your life, you can unlock immense fulfillment and make a meaningful impact in your own life and the lives of others.

T - TRUE REALITY

So, here you are

Imagining and justifying to yourself that what you do makes a difference, while knowing that it is meaningless and unfulfilling.

Imagine five to ten years from now, your life remains mostly unchanged. You follow the same routine, live with the same limitations, and your innate desire to lead a fulfilling life remains unfulfilled. Without taking any action to improve it, your future will merely echo your present. While you may advance in your job title, acquire more possessions, and accumulate more wealth than you have now, your core self may remain unchanged.

You will continue the path you are on feeling, maybe 5x more

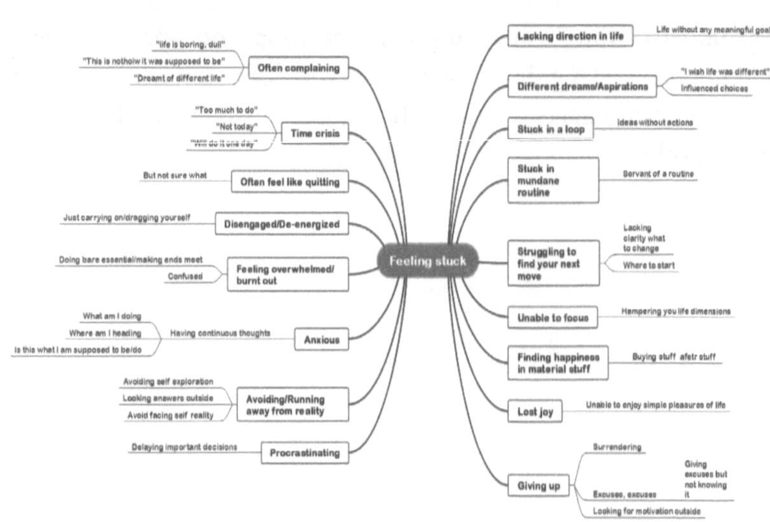

How would this make you feel? Will you be able to endure a life of personal (not evolving or growing personally in terms of personal development and self-awareness) and mental stagnancy (not experiencing intellectual and cognitive growth), or do you have a burning desire to transform your reality?

"True reality" is an honest assessment of your life, having awareness of the gaps between your current and desired reality, or as Stoics say, "being in good terms with your highest self."

It is about where you stand in relation to your life's purpose and goals and what is out of harmony.

The purpose of understanding your true reality is as follows:

- Establishes a baseline or reference point to gauge how far your destination is from your current position and to evaluate whether your actions are truly leading to progress. If not, then you need to change your strategy.
- Gaining clarity and information about where you stand can help you make informed decisions and take actions that align with your aspirations. It enables you to identify any gaps or areas that require attention and improvement.
- Identifying your strengths and weaknesses allows you to leverage your strengths and address any weaknesses.

Have you ever witnessed a symphony orchestra performance? The orchestra comprises various instruments – percussion, brass, strings, and woodwinds, all working together to create a masterpiece. Even a single out-of-tune note can disrupt the entire composition. Similarly, our lives have many interconnected dimensions that need to work together. To lead a happy, balanced, fulfilling, and meaningful life, you need all those aspects to work in perfect harmony, but seldom do we see it.

You might be thinking that you are working hard toward your life's purpose and goals, but the reality could be totally different. Most of us are busy living life on autopilot, running after the wrong goals, doing everything that comes our way, and not what we truly want. We are busy with our daily routines and everything else except sparing some time to self-assess our reality. Whether we agree or not, most of us have been ignoring our reality, and doing so will not change our life, no matter how hard we try.

Life is at its best when every component works together in perfect harmony.

We all talk about living a healthy and balanced lifestyle, at least most of us do. This involves physical and mental well-being, maintaining strong and healthy relationships, advancing in our careers, etc. However, in reality, most of us invest disproportionately in just one aspect, maybe career, finance, or relationships, thereby neglecting other aspects that are key to a balanced life. This results in living an unintentional life, a life lived on autopilot. You may want something but are focusing on limited aspects or none, leaving a huge gap between your "As Is" current state and your "To Be" desired state.

Gaining this clarity to identify the gaps will help you make informed decisions thereafter.

You want to have a healthy and balanced lifestyle. You decide to self-assess your current reality and reflect on various key aspects of your life like:

Physical health: You can barely dedicate time to exercise and maintain an inconsistent diet.

Relationships: You have been neglecting some important relationships (friends, family, romantic partners) due to your busy schedules. You understand that these relationships are important; however, you are focused on other priorities.

Career: You have a stagnant career, not pursuing growth opportunities or leveraging your skills and passion.

Assessing your reality and taking steps to align your actions with your goals, you can gradually create a more balanced and fulfilling life. The self-awareness gained from this understanding of your current position allows you to make intentional choices that support overall well-being and get closer to living the life you envisioned.

Taking an honest look at your life and assessing whether your actions are aligned with your goals is an important part of personal growth and development. By recognizing areas that may be working against your goals or being mindful of limiting beliefs and mindsets, you can make adjustments and take proactive steps to create a more fulfilling and purposeful life.

Remember, self-awareness and a willingness to continuously evaluate and realign your actions with your purpose and goals can lead to a more meaningful and balanced life.

Meet Mark, a 40-year-old professional who has been working in a corporate job for several years. On the surface, Mark appears successful, but deep down, he feels unfulfilled and lacks clarity of passion and purpose. He realizes that he is living a life dictated by external expectations and societal norms rather than pursuing what truly matters to him.

Through self-reflection and introspection, Mark gains clarity. He recognizes that his current job, although stable and financially rewarding, does not align with his true interests and values. He aspires to make a positive impact on society and feels a strong desire to pursue a career in environmental sustainability, a field he has always been passionate about. He understands there is a need for it, and he has the relevant skills as he has a degree in environmental sciences.

Mark also realizes that he has been neglecting his personal well-being. Due to work demands and a busy lifestyle, he has been ignoring his physical and mental health, which has resulted in stress and a lack of work-life balance.

By becoming aware of his reality, Mark understands the reasons behind his dissatisfaction and lack of fulfillment. He acknowledges that he has been prioritizing external success and societal expectations over his own desires. He recognizes that to live a more balanced and fulfilling life, he needs to make significant changes.

With this newfound clarity, Mark can take actions to realign his life with the purpose and values that he seeks.

> *"First say to yourself what you would be; and then do what you have to do" - Epictetus*

In Stoic philosophy, the ultimate goal of life aligns with Aristotle concept of Eudaimonia, which encompasses holistic well-being. It's not fleeting happiness but a sustained state of contentment.

> *"Dig within. Within is the wellspring of Good; and it is always ready to bubble up, if you just dig." - Marcus Aurelius*

Stoics believed that nature wants us to be the best version of ourselves, and so we have it in our natural potential. Eudaimonia refers to overall happiness and not just temporary moments of happiness. When you are happy overall, then each moment will also reflect that.

To achieve Eudaimonia, you need to live with:
- Arete – Arete is an ancient Greek word meaning excellence or virtue. The pursuit of excellence requires a focus on the quality of actions. Actions in harmony with our vision and values. Getting a dream job or earning a million dollars may give you temporary happiness in the short run. Happiness and fulfillment

occur when you bridge the gap between where you want to be and where you are through conscious actions that support your purpose.

- Focus on what you control – What's beyond our power is not important for our flourishing. Not everything is in your control, but your behavior, attitude, and actions are. Make choices to control your life and not be controlled by it.

"The opponent within one's own head is more formidable than the one on the other side of the net." - Timothy Gallwey.

You have control over your game and not the opponents. Stop being a victim and be in control of your choices, actions, behavior, and attitude to take on life's challenges.

- Take responsibility – Taking ownership of our choices and consequences and being accountable for our actions. Life is now. The past is gone, and the future is a mystery, and you are responsible for how you design your future.

Success depends on acknowledging and being aware of your true reality and taking actions to change it to fulfill your purpose in life.

Happiness is about doing things but with the awareness of how your actions are aligned with your purpose.

"If a man knows not which port he sails; no wind is favourable" *Lucius Annaeus Seneca*

Life Assessment and Gap Analysis

Objective: to assess and evaluate your current life situation ("As Is" reality) and compare it to your desired reality ("To Be" reality). By identifying the gaps between the two, you can prioritize areas for improvement and develop an action plan to align your life with your purpose and goals.

Instructions:
- Begin by reflecting on the question: "Where are you?" in relation to your desired reality or the profound insights you've attained

through gaining a clear understanding of your passions and life's purpose. Consider your aspirations and all the aspects discussed before.

- Assess your current reality by evaluating different aspects of your life, such as career, relationships, health, personal growth, finance, and others. List these aspects in a table or template. You could also do it at an overall "life" level, but remember, the gaps that you identify would still relate to one of those aspects.
  - You may use the following questions to identify gaps:
  - Where are you & Where do you need to be?
  - Why do you need it?
  - What do you need to have?
  - What do you need to do?
  - What needs to be different?
  - How are you going to fill the gaps?
  - Assign a score on a scale of 1 to 10 for each aspect to indicate its alignment with your desired reality. Use the following scale:

1: No alignment
5: Moderate alignment
10: High alignment

- For each aspect, write a brief explanation of why you assigned that score. This will help you gain insights into the reasons behind the current level of alignment or none.

Aspect	Alignment Score	Explanation

- Consider the aspects that are key to your desired reality. Identify three aspects in order of priority based on their importance and how much they are lagging behind.
- Identified Key Aspects (Priority Order):

Aspect 1: [Explain the current alignment level and why there is a gap]

Aspect 2: [Explain the current alignment level and why there is a gap]

Aspect 3: [Explain the current alignment level and why there is a gap]

- Visualize where you want to be in each aspect and write a brief description of your ideal alignment for each one. This will help you set clear goals for improvement.

- Conduct a gap analysis by comparing the current alignment scores with your ideal alignment for the three prioritized aspects. Identify the aspects with significant gaps, as these are the areas that require your significant attention and improvement.

- Finally, based on the identified gaps, outline the actions or changes needed to bridge those gaps and align your life with your purpose and goals. Write down specific actions or strategies to fill the gaps.

Aspect	Current State "As Is"	Desired State "To Be"	Gaps	Actions

Here's an example to explain the Life Assessment and Gap Analysis process:

"Where are you?" in relation to your desired reality.

My desired reality is to have a fulfilling career, maintain healthy relationships, prioritize personal well-being, and achieve financial stability.

- Assess your current reality:

Aspect	Score	Explanation
Career	4	Feel stuck in my current job and not progressing towards my long-term goals. It's monotonous and doesn't provide any opportunity to learn and do something outside the job role.
Relationship	7	I have strong relationships with friends and family, but I could invest more time and effort. Mostly focusing on the job leaving me no time for pursuing better relations.
Mental Well-being	5	Experience occasional stress and anxiety, affecting my overall mental well-being.
Physical Well-being	5	Engage in some physical activity but not regularly, need to improve my fitness level to take part in Marathon
Personal Growth	3	Haven't actively pursued personal development opportunities aligned with passion.
Finances	5	Though managing my finances okay, but I desire greater stability and financial freedom.

You can break Relation to Family, Friends, Love

- Identify key aspects for improvement. Rank based on priority (1 being the highest priority):
  a) Career
  b) Personal Growth
  c) Health
- GAP analysis

Aspect	"As Is"	GAP	"To Be"
Career	Feel stuck in my current job and not progressing towards my long-term goals. It's monotonous and doesn't provide any opportunity to learn and do something outside the job role.	1. No opportunities to learn and grow 2. Repeated tasks (monotonous) 3. Limited networking with other professionals and teams 4. Don't feel passionate about what I do, isn't challenging enough.	Fulfilling job that aligns with my passions and offers personal growth and development opportunities.
Personal Growth	Haven't actively pursued personal development opportunities recently.	1. No opportunities to learn and grow 2. Having doubts about self-capabilities in trying something new 3. Lack of clear goals and actions not aligned to aspirations 4. Time management	Personal Growth Continuous learning and personal development to enhance skills and broaden knowledge
Health	Mental Well-being - Experience occasional stress and anxiety, affecting my overall mental well-being. Physical Well-being - Engage in some physical activity, but I need to improve my fitness level to take part in Marathon	1. Awareness and understanding of mental health issues 2. Having a support system 3. Time to do physical exercises 4. Sedentary lifestyle (desk job) 5. Unhealthy dietary habits 6. Preventive care 7. Partner in sports/exercises	Mental Well-being Positive mindset, emotional resilience, and effective stress management techniques. Physical Well-being Optimal physical fitness through regular exercise and a balanced lifestyle.

- Actions to Bridge the Gaps:
  - Career:
    - Seek opportunities for additional training and education, both internally and externally.
    - Enroll in a coaching and mentor program.
    - Network with professionals in desired fields.
    - Take part in projects outside of my domain.

- Personal Growth:
  - Enroll in online courses or workshops.
  - Read self-improvement books.
  - Set specific learning goals.
  - Manage time well by identifying unproductive activities and reducing them.
  - Gain clarity and define life/career goals.
- Well-being:
  - Practice mindfulness and meditation.
  - Seek therapy or counseling support.
  - Develop a self-care routine.
  - Establish a regular exercise routine.
  - Improve dietary habits.
  - Prioritize rest and recovery.

- Actions to Bridge the Gaps: track, and measure your progress as you take actions to bridge the identified gaps

I - IMPEDIMENTS

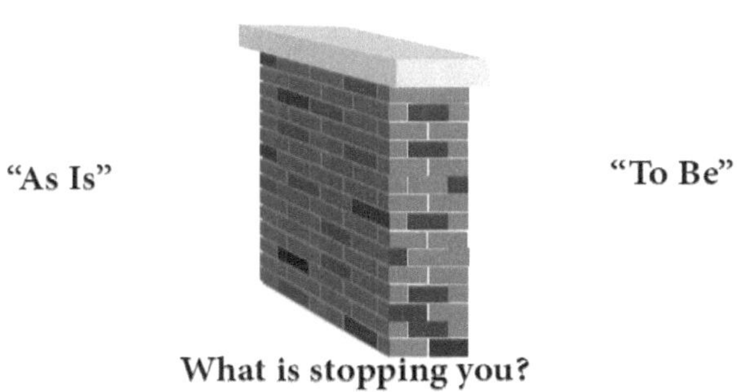

What's Holding You Back? It's a classic conundrum, and the answer is simple: none other than you!

Impediment - "Hindrance or obstruction in doing something"

Obstacles and challenges are a natural part of life, and they often stand in the way of us living our finest life. It is important to recognize that we are often our own biggest hindrance or obstruction when it comes to achieving our goals. These self-imposed barriers have the potential to hinder and even extinguish our aspirations, acting as barriers that prevent us from reaching our full potential and living our dreams. It is crucial to be aware of and acknowledge these limitations in order to overcome them and pursue our aspirations with determination and resilience.

Setting goals is one thing, but taking the necessary actions to achieve them requires significant effort and perseverance.

Take a moment to reflect on your resolutions from the past years. How many have you accomplished, and how many have you carried over from previous years? Over 90% of these goals remain unfulfilled.

It is common for many of our goals to remain unfulfilled, and we may find ourselves repeating those goals year after year. I recall having "quit smoking" on my list for years, until that changed one significant day in 2020 when I finally crossed it off for good.

When we embark on our journey towards our goals, we often begin with optimism and visions of success. However, along the way, we often encounter obstacles that cause us to stumble. It is at this point that many people give up on their goals.

Reflecting on my own struggle to quit smoking, every cigarette seemed to be the "last one" until I picked up the next one. External factors like stress and even emotions would trigger the urge. That's just an excuse to convince and justify our actions. I am stressed so I need a smoke, I am excited so I need one. Apparently, study[2] suggests that our brain does not distinguish between excitement and anxiety, so in any mood it would give a signal to smoke.

Embracing challenges for personal growth

Challenges, obstacles, and hurdles are an integral part of human life. While they can be demanding and sometimes even tough to overcome, they play a crucial role in our personal growth and development. At the same time, life without them would be dull and boring, with complacency obscuring the potential that lies ahead. They serve as catalysts for progress, pushing us out of our comfort zones and encouraging us to tap into our full potential.

Imagine yourself cruising on a highway without any twists or turns – it might appear smooth and effortless, but the thrill of the unknown, the exhilaration of conquering obstacles, would be missing. The journey would become monotonous and uninspiring. Bends and inclines keep us engaged and attentive; challenges demand our focus and resilience.

---

[2] Study published in the journal Nature Neuroscience in 2013

Embracing the Chaos for Growth:

No one sets goals to fail, but when obstacles come in the way, some change course, and some give up. The moment these obstacles and challenges strike, we are in a state of chaos.

Ever wondered why some people are successful and some are not? What is it that they have which others don't? Well, Nothing!

They don't have anything different; the difference lies in their ability to embrace chaos and continuously improve themselves and their tactics to achieve the desired results. Chaos is nothing to be afraid of; in fact, it is during the state of chaos that one can truly determine their capabilities and, above all, refine their strategy to overcome their limitations. Remember, no matter how carefully you planned in advance, there will be obstacles.

This reminds me of a conversation between a captain and his executive officer in the movie "Crimson Tide." During a disagreement about running a mock preparedness drill on a submarine under the threat of enemy fire, the captain says, "Confusion on the ship is nothing to fear. It should be taken advantage of. You don't just fight battles when everything is hunky-dory."

You don't just plan for things going well; you also need to acknowledge the fact that things will not always go as per the plan and strategize accordingly. With that level of understanding of obstacles and challenges, we can better equip ourselves to overcome them.

Reflect on the obstacles you have encountered in the past, in pursuit of your goals. Consider the following questions:

- What are some of the obstacles or challenges you have faced in the recent past?
- How did you initially respond to these obstacles?
- Did you adapt your strategies or give up on your goals?
- What have you learned from these experiences?
- How can you better plan for obstacles in the future?

Often, limitations and obstacles stem from various sources. They can be external, such as societal expectations, financial constraints, or lack of resources, support, and opportunities. They can also be internal, arising from self-doubt, fear of failure, or a fixed mindset. Regardless of their origin, limitations can hold us back and prevent us from taking the necessary steps towards our aspirations. It is essential to recognize whether these limitations are within our control or external factors beyond our influence. In many cases, we may find ourselves grappling with circumstances and situations that we cannot change or directly influence. If that's the case, it's important to acknowledge there's little we can control and stressing about them is ultimately futile.

The first step in overcoming limitations is to identify and understand them. Remember, your limitations do not define you. They are challenges that can be conquered with perseverance, determination, and a belief in your own potential. By confronting and overcoming these limitations, you can unlock your true self and live a life that aligns with your deepest desires.

It's important to recognize the hindrances or obstacles that can prevent us from living our finest life. Here are some common factors that can impede our progress:

1. Focus on the end and not the journey – It is common to get excited about the end goal, and we are so eager to reach the end. Yet, it's also crucial to remember that individual small steps lead to the desired objective. We give up because we overwhelm ourselves by taking giant leaps and not breaking them into manageable chunks. We get so focused on the final destination that we forget the significance of each step and the valuable experiences gained along the journey. Sometime around 2004 or 2005, I started looking for flying schools for training. As I shared earlier, I had always wanted to be a pilot, but I got stuck in a desk job. I didn't hate that job, but I still wanted to fly. I started looking for alternatives.

It was during that time I discovered that there are other possibilities like paragliding and hang gliding. That would be fun. So, I started searching for schools and came across a few. I began communicating with them and finally chose to get trained with one of them. You see, the reason I chose that particular school and not others was because of their practical approach to the journey of learning. I realized it later, but the fact was that whoever I was interacting with, I expressed my desire to become a paragliding instructor and wanted to be trained for that. This was the time when I had never even witnessed a paraglider in action or even seen a paraglider. I was kind of consistent in that message, so focused on becoming one that I didn't even contemplate the numerous courses and countless hours of flying that lay ahead.

It was only when one of the instructors responded, and that changed my perspective. He pointed out that I hadn't even started the journey and experienced it, yet all I was thinking of was becoming an instructor. I needed to experience that first flight, which might reveal whether this path was truly meant for me or not. That was the moment when I understood the importance of taking one step at a time, rather than fixating solely on the end goal. So, I got trained to become a paraglider pilot but not an instructor. I took to the skies at my leisure, cherishing each flight. This adventure taught me the significance of savoring each moment and recognizing that the journey itself is priceless.

2. Fear of Failure – Many times, we fail to act because of the fear of failure. You want to do something, but the fear of things going horribly wrong grips you, so you don't do what you are supposed to do or want to do. Often, the fear is not about the challenge but about the consequences of failure, which could be embarrassment, shame, disappointing others, loss of self-esteem. Our brain is designed to protect us from doing things that are uncomfortable, scary, and difficult. Whenever a situation arises, it will find the best and easiest possible solution for us, which is usually not taking

action to get into the uncomfortable situation or taking the easy way out. These are thinking practices and habits that are formed with years of experience.

I was feeling stuck in my career, doing the same stuff day in and day out. I would go to the office every day and get drained out not just physically, but mentally as well. I knew I had to do something different. I thought of venturing out into entrepreneurship, starting something of my own, so I contemplated some ideas which I liked and were relevant. However, I couldn't take that all the way because I was afraid of failure. I came from a service background and was in a job for close to fifteen plus years, so I was afraid that I would fail.

I was good at research, so I gathered a lot of data supporting my ideas and even went ahead and created a plan. I spoke with some people, yet I gave up when the execution part was due. Now, after so many years, I am on my own. Though I am not working on my original idea, that's still in the parking bay and not yet dead. While the fear of failure is real, it's possible to overcome it by focusing on strengths, being resourceful, and taking steps towards personal growth and development, most importantly taking consistent actions.

3. Self-Doubt - When was the last time you wanted to do something and stopped yourself from doing it, thinking it's crazy, not possible, way out of your league? It occurs when you doubt your capabilities or lack confidence. It keeps you stuck where you are. Overcoming self-doubt involves challenging negative thoughts, building self-belief, and taking small steps to prove ourselves wrong.

I had this fear of speaking in public, and I thought that I could never do that. Whenever there was an opportunity to speak in front of people, I would always back out. I remember this one incident when I was in school. I don't remember the year, but it was definitely my junior year of school. I decided to participate in a storytelling competition. I was prepared and locked and loaded. The moment I saw the crowd of children from backstage, I vanished!

I was more afraid of what the other children, including my classmates and friends, would think if I didn't narrate it well. But guess what? That still happened because I chickened out. Later in my life, I realized that it was all in my head. Now, not only did I conquer my fears of public speaking, but I also conduct trainings and keep experimenting with it, and guess what? It turned out fine. Who would've thought, right?

Fear/Self-doubt manifests itself in the form of:
- Excuses
- Procrastination
- Hiding
- Anxiety
- Hesitation
- Being hypercritical
- Helplessness

4. Controlling the uncontrollable - Often, we worry about things that are simply beyond our grasp, and usually that's when the screwups happen. You can't control the uncontrollable. Let's say you're an ardent cricket enthusiast. How many times have you stood on the pitch, ball in hand, bowled to the batsman, and the batsman did exactly what you wanted him to do? You may have got it right occasionally, perhaps a wicket or a dot ball. But if every delivery went precisely as planned by the bowler, there would be no fun and suspense in the game as every outcome would be predictable. Sachin Tendulkar wouldn't have become the great batsman he is today, right? But in reality, he's had ups and downs, and that's what makes the game so exhilarating. Life is unpredictable; accept that we can't control everything.

I was working on an improvement project. As part of the project, I had collected a lot of data, which was to be presented to the leaders for project approval. I was making a presentation, but before I could share it with the leaders, I decided to have a discussion with the process owners so that everyone is on the same page. I was in a discussion with one of the process owners explaining the situation in his workflow, and to my surprise (and frustration), he disagreed with the presented facts. I reminded him that this was the official data as shared by his teammates. He still didn't agree, and we got into a bit of an argument, and our egos went high, and my boss had to intervene. Later I realized that I can't control his thoughts and perspective, but what I can control was the accuracy and integrity of the data. Later, the situation was resolved, not by him but his superiors.

5. Comfort zone – We have all built our comfort zones and avoid stepping out of them. It's a shell within which we are at ease, and it minimizes the risk of being stressed out. Our mind is built in a way that it always tries to conserve our energy. It's like a regulator that gets activated as soon as you encounter an uncomfortable situation. That's why bringing change, despite being natural, is so difficult.

I love this quote by Robin Sharma: "The mind is a wonderful servant, but a terrible master." If you let your mind take control, then it will, like an ideal servant, not let you get into any uncomfortable situations. For ages, you have been allowing your mind to push you around. As a result, whenever such a situation arises, all you are left with are more excuses justifying your inactions.

I was out of the corporate world in 2019, but before that, for close to about 3 years, I was stuck in my comfort zone. I was going to offices, having those unending discussions, meetings, most of which were without outcomes. The worst part of it was that I knew it, and yet I was not able to take action. I kept justifying myself that this is safe and continued the same life day after day. And then it finally happened in 2019. I have absolutely no regret about it as I realized what I was missing. I haven't become super-rich yet, and I will be truly honest, I do want to, but more than that, I am happy getting better, learning, and growing each day. This probably wouldn't have been possible if I were still stuck in the same situation. Please note, don't take this as a suggestion to quit your job.

6. Beliefs - Remember, when we were kids, life was so simple. We dreamt about things, and we even made those dreams a reality in our wildly creative imagination. We were a pilot, president, astronaut, doctor, fireman, police officer, Tarzan, Superman, and whatnot. We had no doubts that whatever we thought was not achievable. It seemed like everything was just an arm's length away, and all you needed to do was stretch your arms and get it. Life was amazing, and then reality struck; we grew up. From school to graduation to post-graduation and to a job, and from one job to another, to another, and we just kept growing and growing. Well, they say that with age comes wisdom, but in the current scenario, I am not really sure. I guess, with age, we are now more stuck, more stressed, and more confused.

All of us came into this world with a blank mind, and as we grew older, things changed. We started gathering information from the world around us by witnessing events, people, situations, and experiences of our own and others. We started adding meaning and assumptions to these experiences and drew conclusions for each one of them. Based on our conclusions and understanding of events and situations, we formed beliefs and biases that got ingrained in our memory, and we developed certain behavior patterns and habits. Our reactions to any situation, event, or interaction are based on these beliefs and biases. They got hard-coded into our brains and defined our behavior patterns and habits.

It doesn't matter whether they have served us well or not, but they are there and are a big contributor to what we are today. We can have positive as well as negative or limiting beliefs. The fact is that we live with both, and even though those limiting beliefs are not serving us well, we still don't work towards getting rid of them. In fact, we may not even be aware that they exist and are driving us. To get rid of them, we first need to be aware of them.

Our actions and reactions to most of the things we encounter are based on these hard-coded beliefs and biases we have established over the years.

7. Expectations – Expecting too much from others and yourself often derails the journey when those expectations are not met. When it's others, it's really not in your control, and when it's you, then you are overloading yourself. This journey will have its share of failures, and you will have to take detours many times. You need to improvise and adapt to the changing situation rather than getting discouraged and giving up. The future is uncertain, and situations will change, so should your plans.

We all have a lot of expectations related to career and personal life, most of which don't serve us well, especially when they are not met. They strain our relationships, increase our stress and anxieties, and yet we live with them. I have realized this, and I wouldn't say I am done with them, but I am gradually getting there.

8. Skill – Do you think you have the right skills to make that transformational change that you have decided to work on? Sometimes, a lack of necessary skills or knowledge can impede progress. Identifying the required skills and investing time and effort in acquiring them can empower us to overcome obstacles and achieve our goals.

Remember Murphy's law: "Anything that can go wrong will go wrong." What you do when the obstacles strike defines you and the outcome.

Your Show Stoppers:
Imagine you are on a personal development journey, striving to achieve your goals and aspirations. Along the way, you may encounter various obstacles or challenges that have the potential to hinder your progress. These obstacles can come from both external and internal factors, as shared before. To ensure that these obstacles

do not derail your journey, it is important to identify and address them proactively.

Identifying and Prioritizing Obstacles

Objective: This activity helps you pinpoint and tackle the hurdles that might block your path to achieving your goals. By understanding and addressing these obstacles, you'll boost your ability to conquer them and stay on course toward your desired outcomes.

Instructions:

• Create a Mind Map: Begin with your goal at the center. Branch out to obstacles that have hindered you in the past or could potentially do so in the future. Use keywords or short phrases to describe each obstacle. This visual map helps you explore how these obstacles relate to one another and how they impact your journey. Keep building on the mind map by capturing the belief that is behind that obstacle.

Example Mind Map:

In this example, the central idea represents the goal, followed by obstacles people face in transforming their lives, followed by the associated limiting beliefs that often contribute to these obstacles.

The mind map visually captures the interconnectedness of these obstacles, illustrating that they can influence and impact each other. It provides a holistic view of the potential challenges individuals may face, serving as a starting point for further analysis and prioritization.

- Rating and Prioritization Criteria:
  - Controllable: Determine if each obstacle is within your control (Yes = 1) or not (No = 0). Controllable obstacles are those that you have some degree of influence or control over, while uncontrollable obstacles are factors beyond your control. If you have chosen any uncontrollable obstacles, there's no need to continue with those.
  - Severity: Rate the impact of each obstacle on your progress using this scale: 5 = Will halt progress, 4 = Delays, 3 = Partial failure, 2 = Minor nuisance, 1 = Negligible.
  - Likelihood: Evaluate the likelihood of encountering each obstacle using this scale: 5 = Inevitable, 4 = Situational, 3 = Occasional, 2 = Rare, 1 = Unlikely.

- Prioritization:
  - Calculate the score for each obstacle: Controllable * Severity * Likelihood.
  - Identify the obstacle with the highest score; this is your top priority.
  - Develop an action plan to address this obstacle first.
- Action Plan: Create a plan to overcome your top-priority obstacle. Break it down into actionable steps and set a timeline for implementation. Seek support or resources if needed.
- Repeat: Continue this process for other obstacles based on their prioritization scores. Address them one by one.

This activity helps you identify and focus on the most crucial obstacles, increasing your chances of achieving your goals effectively.

Obstacles	Associated Belief	Control	Severity	Likelihood	Score	Action Plan

Beliefs:

Beliefs are deeply held convictions or opinions that individuals hold about themselves, others, and the world around them. These beliefs significantly shape our thoughts, attitudes, behaviors, and decision-making processes. They serve as the filters through which we interpret and make sense of our experiences and perceptions.

We all possess incredible potential to achieve things that may seem beyond our current capabilities. You might be wondering how it is possible to accomplish such feats. Well, the truth is, you can always expand your capabilities. Consider the example of Sir Isaac Newton, the renowned physicist who formulated the law of gravity. Initially, he was just an ordinary individual like you and me. However, through personal development and continuous growth, he unlocked his potential. If Newton had succumbed to his mother's wishes and doubted himself, he would have become a farmer and abandoned his education.

Next time you find yourself feeling stuck or unable to accomplish something, it's crucial to examine your thoughts and beliefs. They can either restrict your possibilities or empower you to achieve extraordinary things beyond imagination.

Beliefs take shape over years through our experiences and how we interpret them, often without conscious awareness. They get coded in our minds for the rest of our lives, unless we consciously try to change them. As time passes, these beliefs begin to shape our lives. If we harbor limiting beliefs, they can hinder us from creating the life we desire.

They operate as a subconscious autopilot, guiding us without conscious realization. Once a belief is formed, the mind works to reinforce those beliefs. We don't change them because we don't realize them, so we live with them for the rest of our lives.

Imagine you're driving a car, and you slam the brakes without realizing it because a ball has rolled onto the road. You didn't intend to brake; your foot simply reacted. That is the influence of subconscious ideas. These beliefs discreetly influence your thoughts and behaviors without you even recognizing it.

It doesn't matter if they've served you well; they're still there and have played a significant role in shaping who you are today.

The power to live the life you want lies in your ability to "think" and "act." It may sound simple, but most of the time, we get stuck at the thinking stage. This tendency becomes a habit over time. The mind is wired to protect us from uncomfortable, scary, or difficult situations.

Your limiting beliefs hold you back and manifest through hesitation, self-doubt, overthinking or being hypercritical, excessive worrying, procrastination, hiding, and fear of failure.

Embracing a belief creates a certain reality for you, and it remains stuck unless you change it.

Our brain operates like a muscle that can be trained through conscious effort. Therefore, it is never too late to change those beliefs that have been holding you back and limiting your possibilities. Beliefs can be altered, and you don't have to wait years to gain new experiences and beliefs. It could happen right now. The key is awareness of these beliefs and how they are disempowering you.

For instance, let's say you want to become a coach, but you believe that you are not good and an introvert in front of strangers. This belief becomes your reality, and you don't even attempt or run away from such situations fixating on your belief.

The first step is identifying these limiting beliefs and assessing how they align with your transformational journey.

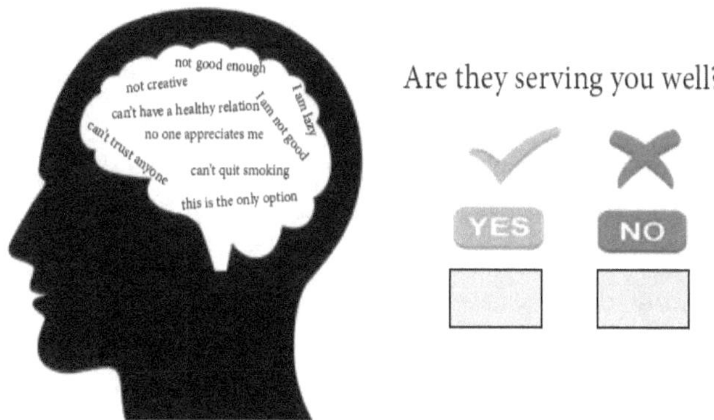

To break free from such limiting beliefs, it is essential to reframe them. Reframing involves altering the way you think about a belief, which opens up numerous possibilities and creates a new perspective. Here are some examples:

- Belief: "I will fail."
- Reframe: "It will be a learning experience."
- Belief: "It's too late for me to change."
- Reframe: "It's never too late to start again."
- Belief: "People hate me."
- Reframe: "They need to know me to like me."

Through reframing, we don't deny reality; rather, we seek a balanced perspective by gathering evidence that supports or challenges an existing belief.

Let's examine your beliefs. You can refer to the "Find your patterns" and "Identify obstacles" exercise where you identified some beliefs that are limiting your progress. By addressing and reframing these beliefs, you can overcome obstacles and unlock your true potential.

Identifying Limiting Beliefs and Reframing

Objective: The objective of this exercise is to identify your beliefs, particularly the ones that are limiting your progress, and to reframe them with more positive and empowering alternatives.

- Your Limiting Beliefs - List your common beliefs—especially those obstructing your progress. (Use the mind map technique or simply document your common beliefs. Write down the beliefs that you often find yourself holding, especially the ones that hinder your progress.)

- Anchor Thoughts - Explore the recurring thoughts reinforcing the belief. Anchor thoughts are the recurring thoughts or self-talk that reinforce the belief and keep it firmly in place. Thoughts or ideas that strongly influence our beliefs and shape our perspectives. They act as mental anchors, holding our beliefs in place and influencing how we perceive ourselves, others, and the world around us.

- Triggers - Identify triggers (situations, people, locations, times, or systems) that tend to activate or reinforce the belief. Describe how each belief makes you feel (e.g., fear, self-doubt, disappointment, overwhelmed, sad, anxious, unworthy, stressed, shame, etc.).

- Source - Reflect on the origin of each belief, such as past experiences, upbringing, societal influence. Identify where and when you first adopted this belief. It will be difficult for some, don't worry if you can't, but try.

- Cost of Belief - Evaluate the consequences of holding each belief in terms of missed opportunities. (Consider the actions you have taken or not taken in the past due to this belief and the potential opportunity or outcomes that you missed out on.)

- Examine Evidence - Examine evidence that supports and contradicts each belief. Look for examples and experiences from your own life that challenge the belief and provide a different perspective. In all likelihood, you would have scenarios when you took actions beyond your limiting beliefs. Maybe not for all, but for many and that itself is an evidence that you can go beyond those beliefs.

- Reframe Beliefs - Generate alternative interpretations or reframes for each limiting belief. Create more positive, empowering, and realistic statements that counteract the limitations of the old belief.
- Rational and Balanced Perspective - Compare the perspectives of the old limiting belief and the reframed belief. (Consider which perspective has more supporting evidence, is more rational, balanced, and aligns with your goals and values.)
- Integration and Practice: Once you've identified the new belief, integrate it into your thinking patterns and daily life. Practice affirming the new belief, repeat it to yourself regularly, and consciously apply it in situations where the old limiting belief would have influenced your thoughts and behaviors.

Limiting Belief	Anchor Thoughts	Trigger	Source	Cost	Evidence	Reframe	Rationale	Action Plan

Example - "Not good enough to start own business."
- Triggers:
  - People: Comparison to successful individuals
  - Situation & Location: being in a professional setting or attending industry-related events.
- Emotions: Self-doubt – doubting self-capabilities, fear: plagued by fear of failure, rejection, stressed: pressure to prove oneself.
- Anchor Thoughts: Not possessing enough expertise to venture into entrepreneurship successfully. Lacking expertise since one is from a service background.
- Source: Growing up, repeatedly exposed to the notion that starting a business is risky and only a select few with money, status, and a vast network can truly succeed.
- Cost of Belief: Missing out on valuable opportunities for personal growth, financial independence, and fulfillment.

Remaining trapped in unfulfilling jobs or stagnant career paths, denying self the chance to explore entrepreneurial potential.

- Examine Evidence: Despite reservations, there would be individuals with similar skills and knowledge successfully launching their own businesses. They may have also taken on projects that showcased their abilities and achieved positive results, demonstrating their competence.
- Reframe Beliefs: "I can develop my capability and start my own venture" acknowledge the capacity to learn and grow along the way, viewing each challenge as an opportunity for development and success.
- Evaluate Evidence & Rational and Balanced Perspective: Reflecting on accomplishments as project manager, for example, the successful completion of multiple projects from scratch and the positive feedback received from both superiors and subordinates. This evaluation serves as a validation of abilities and counteract the belief that one is not good enough.
- Integration and Practice: Affirmations, seek feedback, celebrate small victories, reminding myself of evidence supporting reframed beliefs and interpretations.

When we hold limiting beliefs, it means that our thinking patterns have become distorted or biased, leading to negative or unhelpful interpretations of ourselves, others, and the world. Reframing is a technique used to challenge and modify these limiting beliefs by introducing alternative, more realistic, and empowering perspectives.

Now, based on the above example and reframed belief, don't expect everything to be a smooth sailing going ahead. Challenges and failures will still be part of the journey, but the difference lies in confronting these hurdles with a positive attitude and strong self-belief as the individual works towards their entrepreneurial goals.

O - DESIGN OPTIONS

This is the phase where you explore and generate potential options based on all the information you have gathered so far following the framework. This is where you ideate to design options that align with your aspirational life.

Ultimately, it's all about options – the ones that you choose and act upon. It has always been your choice, but unfortunately, situations, circumstances, or people often take over and make that decision for you, and all you do is comply.

When designing your life, keep in mind that the destination is fixed, which is your vision, but the options to reach that destination may vary. You have a choice of following the most apparent choice, which is following the herd, or designing your own path.

Imagine your life as a grand journey towards a specific destination, like the peak of a mountain you're eager to ascend, representing your ultimate goal. While the destination remains unchanged, the paths to ascend that mountain are numerous. Each path offers distinct challenges and experiences. Designing these paths symbolizes the options you have while crafting your journey. You could choose to walk the trails or drive to the top using the comfortable roads – these would be the apparent paths for most to follow. On the other hand, you have the power to design your own path, to imagine walking through unexplored terrain.

We possess the power to chart our course through this journey. It can either be the well-accepted path or us venturing into uncharted territory.

"Don't stop the pursuit of your aspirations because of your limitations."

Often, we feel limited in our options or believe that one alternative is the only one accessible, so we choose the most obvious one. Is it, however, the only option?

It's because we've been conditioned our entire lives to think and act in a specific manner, rather than exploring and building our own paths to attaining our goals and having a satisfying existence.

How many of us take the first available job, justifying it as the best option that exists, simply because we're frustrated in our current one? Honestly, I too have fallen prey to this, learning the hard way by choosing options that were even more unfavorable. Sometimes, if you're lucky, you may get another chance and you may take it up, taking a leap of faith, only to find out it's no different.

Think back to the time when you selected your college, undergraduate, or postgraduate course. What made you make that decision? Peer pressure, parental expectations, or teachers and mentors urging you toward careers like becoming a doctor, engineer, lawyer, or pursuing other popular courses. What was the definition of success as taught?

This happened because we were never encouraged to explore and innovate in our life paths; instead, we ended up living up to others' expectations and following the obvious path.

The problem we have in our system is characterized by a one-dimensional approach, where students are taught to follow the same old pattern every year. Repetitive tasks and annual exams with the primary aim of attaining top grades have been the norm for ages and have stifled creativity, unique thinking, and idea generation. This approach is not helping students explore and develop skills that will enable them to live their aspirational and fulfilling lives.

The yearly repetition of similar subjects and examination patterns discourages students from pursuing other endeavors outside the established curriculum. As this continues, a child's unique thought process starts to diminish. Instead of being curious, asking questions, challenging assumptions, and exploring other perspectives, they start conforming. Academically, they may turn out to be good students, but they lack the skills to think innovatively, adapt to dynamic challenges, and pursue their passions.

We've already established that if you love doing something, there's a need for it, and you possess the necessary skills, everything you deserve will follow. The key is capturing the world's attention.

Think back to your vision of an aspirational life. Could you have turned that vision into a lucrative pursuit?

"The secret to happiness in life design isn't making the right choice; it's learning to choose well" (from the book "Design Your Life" by Bill Burnett and Dave Evans).

The choices we make define the path we take in life, and what could be worse than walking on a path that wasn't meant for us?

Imagine wanting to go to Destination "A" but, inadvertently, finding yourself at Destination "B" without the option to backtrack. You can restart, but most people don't.

Remember when you were kids; the possibilities were limitless. As we grew up, our options became limited, more limited, and finally, limited to where we are today.

To create a fulfilling life for yourself, it's crucial to explore alternate paths and possibilities and choose the one that aligns with your purpose and is fueled by your passion, if not entirely so.

Options are all about the choices you make to get on the path toward your fulfilling life and move forward toward achieving it, with an understanding of your limitations. We already understand our goal, our reality, and our limitations.

By exploring different options, we can expand our thinking and challenge our assumptions. We're so accustomed to our standard thinking patterns that we rarely question the standard solutions. Most of the time, the optimal solution lies outside the so-called boundaries or assumptions. If it were within those boundaries, we would already be living our dream life. The reality is that we're still in the process of figuring out how to achieve it.

When I say "explore," I mean going beyond the obvious, or as some may say, thinking outside the box. This enables us to break free from conventional choices and discover new, possibly innovative ones. It opens up a world of possibilities and allows us to find optimal solutions that we may not have considered before. Try this:

Connect the 9 dots using 4 lines without repeating lines and without lifting your pen or pencil

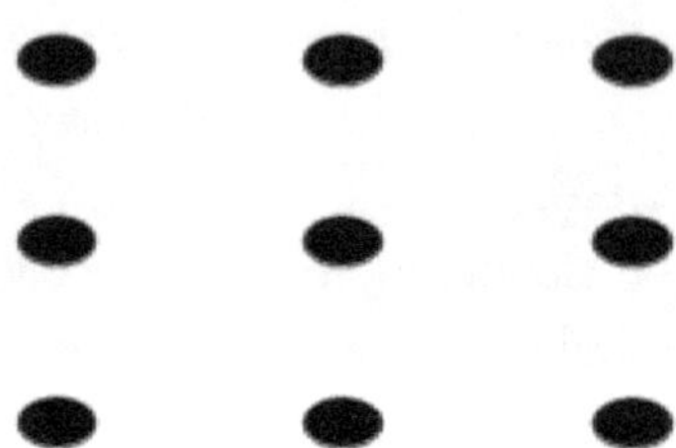

So, if you go with your assumptions and boundaries, then it's impossible to solve this because you will be trying hard within those 9 dots, however if you break those boundaries then there might be multiple options to solve.

We need to choose the path that is effective and aligned with our objectives. It's about making informed decisions that are most likely to lead us to the desired outcomes.

While choosing the right option is critical in this journey, what is equally important is taking action. Opportunities alone are not enough. They will remain distant possibilities unless you take action. Options are not just about finding ways to reach your goal but also ensuring that they are doable and that you take action on them.

Have you ever had an idea about something or encountered a problem and didn't take any action, only to see someone else implement it later? Often, we miss out on opportunities due to self-imposed barriers that obstruct us.

A while back, I had an idea and worked on it for some time but failed to take action to execute it. A year later, I saw that idea being implemented by someone else. I realized that if you don't act on your ideas, someone else will.

In life, we create boundaries for ourselves that we seldom cross. These are imaginary lines that we've drawn around ourselves, and crossing them doesn't require much effort. Cultivating options and seizing them challenges the mind's reluctance. Your mind will play tricks on you, discouraging you from taking the step. Remember, It doesn't want you to face uncomfortable situations, such as rejection, making mistakes, or appearing foolish in others' eyes. This can lead to self-doubt, hesitation, fear of failure, procrastination, and more. The real test is whether you can overcome these feelings, come up with ideas, and take action to execute them. If you can do that, you've conquered those obstacles.

Now, when I say the mind dissuades you from taking action, I don't mean it's the villain. It does so because you've programmed it with your beliefs and biases.

A few years back, I found myself in an unexpected situation - my first consulting assignment. I hadn't actively been seeking such opportunities. After more than a decade of working in traditional jobs, I received an offer for this assignment. Initially, I hesitated. Even though I had experience leading projects and providing internal consultations, this was my first venture into external consulting for a client I hadn't worked with before.

My mind played all sorts of tricks on me: "What if they don't like my work?" "What if I mess up?" I wasn't entirely convinced because consulting independently was significantly different from being in a job. The stakes were higher, dealing with a new set of people with whom I had no prior interaction, and the expectations were elevated. I had to be crystal clear about those expectations. I could have easily turned down the opportunity, and honestly, I had nothing to lose. When these situations arise, most of us tend to retreat to our comfort zones. Instead of focusing on taking the leap, we start searching for reasons not to seize the opportunity. I had dozens of those reasons, believe me.

But this is where the saying "move it or lose it" comes into play. So, I moved forward. Whether the client would ultimately be satisfied with my work was not entirely within my control. However, what I could control was my approach. I decided to embrace the experience, learn from it, give it my best effort, and gain a thorough understanding of their requirements and expectations. Amidst hesitation and self-doubt, I accepted the assignment. By staying focused on the assignment's objectives and working diligently, I not only met but exceeded their expectations, and my work was highly appreciated.

In this phase of designing options, we are in the process of ideating, exploring, and ultimately selecting the best design option that aligns with our passion and purpose, enabling us to live our aspirational life.

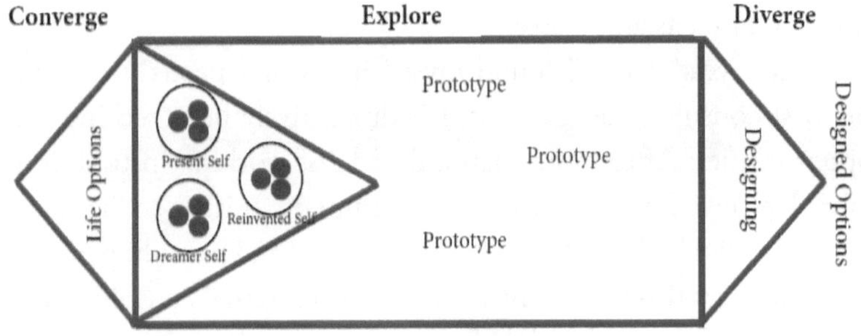

Exploring Life Options Aligned with Passion and Purpose

Objective: To generate ideas and explore different life options[3] that resonate with your passion and purpose, ultimately leading to the selection of the most suitable option for living your aspirational life.

Exploration:
- Set up a quiet and comfortable space for idea generation.
- Gather materials: Paper, pens, and a whiteboard or flip chart.

---

[3] Inspired by 'Designing your Life' by Bill Burnett & Dave Evans. Adapted and built upon a concept to suit the context of my book.

- Begin the activity by creating three distinct life option maps: "Present Self," "Reinvented Self," and "Dreamer Self." Each option represents a different career path aligned with your passion and purpose.
- You can refer to the "Discovering Your Patterns" exercise while doing this.

Map 1: "Present Self" Option

- Document all ideas that come to your mind regarding your current occupation.
- Describe what currently engages, excites, and energizes you in that.
- Write down specific tasks, roles, or undertakings that align with your current interests and skills.
- Consider how you can enhance or modify your current work, incorporating these roles, tasks to make it more fulfilling and recurrent.

Map 2: "Reinvented Self" Option

- Imagine a scenario where your current pursuit is not an option.
- Design an alternate path—what you would do if your current path or occupation didn't exist.
- Identify new tasks, roles, or undertakings that you would be willing to pursue.
- Explore different possibilities that align with your interests and values.

Map 3: "Dreamer Self" Option

- Envision a life where financial, societal, or parental constraints don't exist.
- Design your ideal career, driven by long-held passions and desires.
- Identify activities, roles, projects, or undertakings that have always fascinated you and that you would love to pursue.

- Consider how you can make a sustainable living from this option if external factors were not obstacles.
- After completing the three mind maps, step back and review the options you have identified.
- Evaluate each option based on your passion, purpose, and alignment with your desired aspirational life.
- Consider the feasibility, potential challenges, and opportunities associated with each option.
- This activity will help you generate ideas and explore various options, allowing you to choose the one that resonates most with your passion and purpose for living your aspirational life.

Reflection and Decision:

Pick the ideas from each map that stand out and you feel good about, and resonates with who you are. Incorporate those and describe them as a doable option. And if being wild and crazy works for you, go-ahead, pick-up ideas collectively from all the maps.

- Reflect on the three options based on their significance and alignment with your aspirational life.
- Evaluate each option based on factors such as "Emotional connect," "Likeability," "Alignment to purpose," "Realistic," "Confidence," "Resources," and "Willing to take risk." You can assign scores from 1 to 5 or apply weighted scoring.
- Select the most suitable and compelling option that resonates with your passion and purpose.
- Visualize and imagine yourself living that option, experiencing the fulfillment and joy it brings.

George is a marketing professional who has been doing the same job for over a decade and is now feeling unfulfilled in his current job because as he grew up the hierarchy, his passion for writing has gotten lost in his job. He gets no time to write what he really loves, which was the reason he became a marketing professional. He aspires for a life where he has flexibility, fulfillment, meaning by living his passion and purpose.

He starts exploring different career options that are aligned with his passion for writing and his purpose of making a positive impact on people's lives through his writing.

- He sets up a quiet and comfortable space.

"Present self":

- He writes down all the activities he is involved in, such as managing budgets, managing campaigns, budgets, reviewing products, writing product descriptions, etc.
- Build on the points that relate to writing aspects and he finds fulfilling.
- Explores ideas on how he can transition to focus more on what he loves by pursuing freelance writing opportunities, blogging, etc.

Title: Engaging in Writing Opportunities

Description: "Leverage current marketing expertise to explore and engage in more writing-centric tasks. Transition the career to focus more on writing, such as pursuing freelance writing projects or personal blogging."

The "Reinvented self" scenario where marketing is not an option:

- He writes down options where he can write articles, stories, etc.
- Building on these ideas, the idea of writing a book or maybe becoming a writing coach, or teaching, etc.

Title: Pursue Creative Writing and Coaching

Description: "A career shift as a freelance writer to fully immerse in creative writing endeavors. Explore writing articles, stories, and essays on topics passionate about. Consider opportunities to provide writing coaching and support to aspiring writers."

The "Dreamer self" option, where money and status are not considerations:

- Becoming a published author and dedicating his life to writing novels that inspire and entertain readers.

- Considers ways to sustain himself financially as an author, such as through book sales, speaking engagements, or teaching writing workshops.

Title: Published Author Inspiring Readers through Novels and Workshops

Description: "Becoming a published author impacting the lives of readers. A life dedicated to writing and publishing novels that inspire and entertain. Considers opportunities to engage with readers through speaking engagements and teaching writing workshops, while ensuring financial sustainability through book sales and related endeavors."

- He then scores each option based on criteria such as likeability, alignment to purpose, realistic feasibility, confidence level, available resources, and willingness to take risks.
- Based on the option that stands out and resonates deeply with him:
- He chooses the "Reinvented self" option of pursuing a career as a freelance writer to build credibility among readers.

Testing Waters

Becoming a freelance writer is a good option for George, but is it the right one? He had three potential career paths in mind, each brimming with promise, but he understood that choosing the right one required more than mere enthusiasm. It's not enough to jump to conclusions or select the first option that seems appealing. A cautionary fact: about 90% of new ventures that start with enthusiasm end up failing to launch. One significant contributor to this failure is the lack of understanding of the complexities involved in those options – a failure to prototype.

Meet Aman, an operations manager for a large corporation. He'd been doing it for about seven years and was very proficient at it. He was done after seven years of doing the same thing every day.

It didn't excite him any longer. He wanted to design his life and do what he had always wanted to do.

Some of his friends encouraged him to pursue his dream, while others suggested sticking with the familiar. Time slipped by, anxiety grew, yet nothing changed.

He literally used to drag himself to work and would frequently take time off, and even when he was at work, he would go through the day with little energy and engagement.

Aman is a computer science engineer and has been keeping himself updated with the changes in technology when he is not working. He has been updating his knowledge specifically in Artificial Learning and is excited about the prospects of the same. He is passionate about technology driving meaningful change. He also loves driving and traveling and dreams of doing an around-the-world solo tour by road, but he is too caught up in the daily routine to even think about it. After graduating, he worked in a tech company for a while before being let go when the company downsized due to market changes. He was then offered a job in a different industry and jumped at the chance.

And so, Aman followed a framework, leading him to three distinct options:

Present Self:

Enroll in courses that Co. demands — Automation — Automate (Current Job)

Job — New one

Courses

A.I. — Present — Dept. Change

Move into I.T. — Different

Coding — I.T. Projects

online Communities — Challenges — within Co. outside — Same Co.

Freelance

'Present Self': Leverage tech skills and Interest. Understanding the potential of A.I., enroll in courses, engage with Communities, Do Side projects to gain knowledge and experience. Move into I.T. department with focus on developing new tech.

The Reinvented Self:

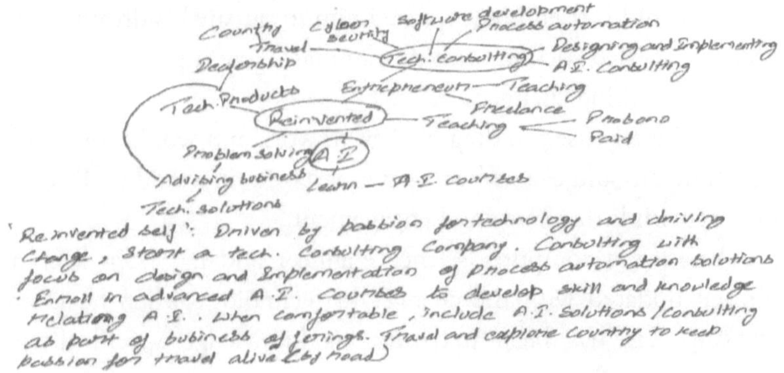

'Reinvented Self': Driven by passion for technology and driving change, start a tech. consulting company. Consulting with focus on design and implementation of process automation solutions. Enroll in advanced A.I. courses to develop skill and knowledge relating A.I.. When comfortable, include A.I. solutions/consulting as part of business offerings. Travel and explore country to keep passion for travel alive (by road)

The Dreamer Self:

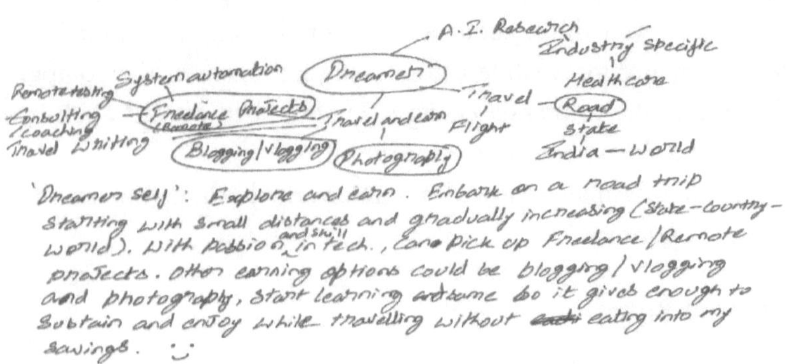

'Dreamer Self': Explore and earn. Embark on a road trip starting with small distances and gradually increasing (State - Country - World). With passion in tech., and skill, can pick up Freelance/Remote projects. Other earning options could be blogging/vlogging and photography. Start learning so it gives enough to sustain and enjoy while travelling without eating into my savings. :)

Following careful contemplation, Aman decided to quit his job and establish a technology consulting business. With his savings, unwavering excitement, and the backing of his loved ones, he moved ahead. Additionally, will travel and explore to pursue his other passion for travelling.

A good start, but within a span of one and a half years, he had to shut down his business. It was not that he chose the wrong option or didn't choose the right one from the other two. He planned it right:

- Conducted thorough market research.
- Established his company.
- Crafted compelling service offerings.
- Cultivated connections with potential clients.
- Managed project acquisition and execution.
- Put effort into upselling and acquiring new clients.

He was doing it right; the only problem was that he didn't prototype. Conversations with subject matter experts, mentors, and immersive experiences were missing links.

Venturing into entrepreneurship necessitates a wide range of skills that contribute to various aspects, especially when you can't afford to hire people with those skills. Skills like entrepreneurial, strategic, financial management, marketing and sales, communication and networking, time management, problem-solving, adaptability, resilience, and some knowledge of legal aspects too. Remember that while possessing these skills is beneficial, you don't need to be an expert in all areas. You can seek guidance, mentorship, and training to develop the necessary skills as your business grows.

The business did well initially, but close to about a year, Aman faced challenges in scaling and managing the company. His tech consulting bit was spot on, and the clients liked his approach. He realized that he lacked certain other skills. He was earning, but not enough, and besides that, more than the work, he was spending time sourcing clients, meeting, documentation, and other related stuff. He had funds which he sourced from his savings, and his wife was earning, but it was just enough, not enough to hire staff in this period. He took on the entire operations right from client identification to sourcing to the delivery of consulting services. He took on too much, and as he moved on, after about a year, instead of being happy, he felt frustrated and struggled to stay afloat.

He made the correct decision, but his tale illustrates the significance of prototyping. While committing to a selected path is admirable, being aware of the journey is essential. Even in your dream life, difficulties and unpleasantness persist. Mental preparation makes a significant difference.

And, of course, you don't want to take the risk of living one life and then rejecting it, living another and keep doing that. Imagine how many years it took for you to realize the current one is not for you.

So, our friend George, who decided to choose the "New Normal" of being a freelance writer, needs to prototype this option by:

- Accumulating practical experience through freelancing or part-time opportunities.
- Networking and collaborating.
- Seeking experienced coaches and mentors in the same line of work.
- Conducting thorough research.
- Developing essential lagging skills.
- Seeking feedback and continually refining.

Prototyping Options

It's like conducting an experiment that will help you gain first-hand experience of all that it takes to live the chosen path, all within a controlled environment. It helps us explore that option and understand not only the good parts but also the nuances involved. It's crucial because it will help you understand what aspects of the work are not aligned with your liking, necessitating proactive strategies to navigate them. Though I have said earlier that "plans can and will fail," having a blueprint to address potential scenarios is much better than being caught unaware.

Remember, I talked about my paragliding experience where I stated that I wanted to be an instructor. At the beginning, it all seemed possible, and I thought I would get trained and then start training people, and that would be so cool. However, as they say, not everything that glitters is gold. Fortunately, my instructor advised me otherwise, and I had the opportunity to gain firsthand insight into the reality of the job. Otherwise, I might have pursued it only to later discover it wasn't the right fit for me.

I'm not saying that I couldn't have done it; in fact, a lot of people have asked me why I didn't pursue it further. The truth is, after gaining a realistic understanding, I am happy keeping it at a hobby level rather than a professional pursuit. I have my glider, I have the other equipment, and I relish the freedom to take flight whenever I wish.

Sometimes, what seems enticing initially may not align with our long-term aspirations. You may like some aspects and dislike others attached to your choice. Yes, of course, you could hire a person, but pursuing a passion doesn't exempt you from aspects you might dislike. My dream was to just fly and not arrange logistics, do marketing, site scouting, and many other things. I wanted to fly, and that's precisely what I did.

I was fortunate that before I invested too much time, money, and other resources, I realized that. Not many are as fortunate. They realize that something is not for them only after they get too deep into it.

I've met numerous individuals who believed they wanted to do something and ended up doing something completely different. It's wiser to explore our interests, uncovering what genuinely resonates with our aspirations.

There are two ways to test that

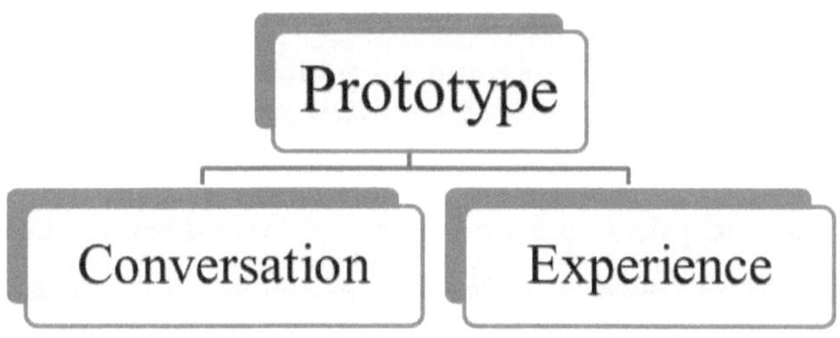

There are two approaches to test and validate life options:

- Through meaningful conversations with subject matter experts (SME's), individuals who are already living that option
- Gaining practical experience through volunteering, interning, or freelancing.

Conversations with SMEs and Individuals Living the Option:

Engaging in conversations with individuals who are already pursuing the options provides valuable insights and first-hand knowledge.

Seek out opportunities to connect with experts in the field or people who have successfully embarked on similar paths. If you don't know anyone, then search for them on the internet. With social media platforms, the world has come closer, making it easy to find people even if they are thousands of miles apart from you. If not individuals, there are communities where like-minded people are always willing to help each other and share experiences. Connect with them to learn about their experiences, challenges, and rewards. Seek their advice and recommendations.

Having these conversations offer unique perspectives, helping you gain a deeper understanding of the option you are testing. If you are lucky, they can also provide valuable guidance and mentorship as you navigate your own journey.

Gaining Practical Experience:

Practical experience is a powerful way to test and validate life options. It allows you to immerse yourself in the field and gain first-hand experience of what it entails. You can consider:

Volunteering: Look for volunteer positions related to the option you are exploring. Non-profit organizations, community initiatives, or industry-specific projects often offer opportunities to contribute your skills and gain hands-on experience. Volunteering allows you to observe and engage in real-world scenarios, build connections, and assess your interest and aptitude for the chosen option.

Internships: Seek opportunities like internships or apprenticeships within organizations or roles that align with your desired option. Internships provide structured learning experiences, allowing you to work alongside professionals, acquire practical skills, and gain insights into the industry's inner workings. They can help you assess if the option is a good fit for you.

Freelancing: Consider freelancing as a way to gain experience and test the viability of an option. Freelancing allows you to offer your services independently, taking on projects and clients in your desired field. This approach provides flexibility and autonomy while giving you a taste of what it's like to work in the chosen domain. It also enables you to build a portfolio, establish a network, and validate your skills and capabilities.

While you are testing, be proactive in seeking feedback from mentors, individuals you are conversing with, and clients. They can provide valuable guidance and help you understand the real picture before you finally commit to it.

Testing your life options is an iterative process. Be open to learning from your experiences, adapting your choices, and embracing new opportunities that may arise along the way. Through testing, you can gather valuable insights, refine your decisions, and ultimately design a fulfilling and purposeful life.

Remember, life's essence lies not in reaching a destination, but in the continuous exploration of options that shape your unique path.

Test Source:

- Create a mind map to kickstart your exploration.
- Begin by documenting all the potential sources you can think of to gather information and test your options.
- Ideate and list different categories such as books, online resources, industry professionals, networking events, online forums, social media groups, etc.

- Expand each category by adding specific sources or individuals that you can explore for insights.

This structured approach will help you systematically gather information and insights as you navigate your journey of testing and validating life options.

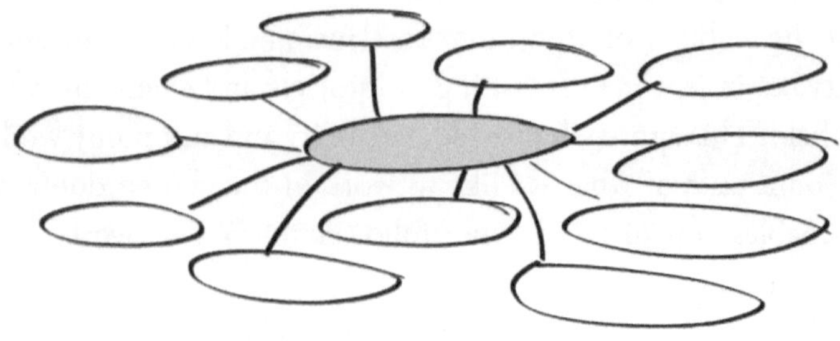

- Determine Relevant Questions:
- Begin by identifying the key questions that you need to ask in order to gather meaningful information about each life option.
- Consider questions such as:
  - What led them to choose this option?
  - What are the day-to-day realities and responsibilities?
  - What skills and knowledge are required?
  - What are the potential obstacles or roadblocks?
  - How do they maintain motivation and overcome challenges?
  - What advice or recommendations do they have for someone starting in this field?
  - Feel free to add more questions if needed, tailored to the specific option you are exploring.
- Seek Interaction:
  - Choose one of the life options you want to test and identify individuals who are already living that option.
  - Reach out to them and request a meeting, whether in person or virtually.

- Arrange a casual setting, such as having coffee or grabbing a drink, where you can engage in a conversation and gather insights about their experiences.
- Gather Insights:
  - During your interaction, make sure to actively listen and take notes to capture key insights and recommendations.
  - Pay close attention to their personal experiences, the challenges they faced, and the rewards they have experienced in their chosen option.
  - Seek practical advice on how to navigate the field, develop the necessary skills, and overcome obstacles.
  - Don't forget to ask for any recommended resources or further contacts to explore.
- Immerse yourself in their journey:
  - Consider shadowing them if the opportunity arises. Spend time closely shadowing them in their daily activities, witnessing their choices and challenges first-hand.
  - Observe their actions, reactions, and interactions.
- Volunteer or Internship:
  - Put yourself in their position mentally, imagining the challenges, emotions, and decisions they face.
- Reflect and Evaluate:
  - Review the information, insights, and experiences you have gathered for each option.
  - Evaluate the feasibility, challenges, and rewards associated with each option based on the insights you have obtained.
  - Consider the compatibility of each option with your skills, interests, and values.
- If required, repeat for Other Options:
  - Once you have gathered insights for one life option, repeat the same process for the other options you want to test.
  - Interact with different individuals who have expertise or experience in those specific options.
  - Engage in conversations, ask relevant questions, and gather insights to compare and evaluate each option.

Let's Go...

Everything that happens to us in life is a result of our choices. Whatever choice you make now will define your tomorrow. Life is all about making choices. Good or bad, but who decides?

YOU!

So, we have come to a stage where you have three choices. This could be quite intimidating. After all, you have put in a considerable amount of time and energy. You have gathered so much information and insights about yourself and developed your options, done soft testing through conversation or experiences, or both. Choosing one and letting go of the others would be difficult. After all, what you do now will impact your life for years.

It's not just about choosing the right option that worries us, but what you do with the other options is actually more worrisome. Many of us agonize about our decisions even years after we have made a decision. Agonizing about whether they made the right decision.

What we are doing is undermining the idea we choose by obsessing over other alternatives. When you are in a soup situation, which I guarantee you will be no matter which option you chose, you will stress over your decisions and wish you had chosen the other one. That won't help; in fact, that will delay the journey as you would spend a lot of energy and time agonizing about the options. In some cases, it might even derail the journey.

Things will go wrong. That doesn't mean that your choice was bad and other options could have avoided that situation. Who knows, it might have avoided that situation, but then you might have to deal with other, maybe even more difficult challenges.

So, what do you do with the options which you didn't choose? Well, you let go of those options. In a crisis, sticking to your initial option you are more likely to doubt and devalue your chosen ones. Known as post decision devaluation effect wherein you focus on the positives of the ones you didn't choose and negatives of the chosen one.

Before letting go, you have to choose one option. That's equally difficult. The best option is often a matter of perspective and time. What might look best for you now may change with a change of circumstances so it's important to be flexible and adaptable. Remember, you choose based on our current understanding and circumstances.

There are two choices:

1. You have gathered information, data, insights about your choices. Choose whatever the data suggests. The problem with this choice is that we are not doing statistical analysis or solving mathematical problems. We are talking about life, and the data is binary; we either like it or not. We have three options, and we like them all. This option doesn't work in our case.

2. We connect with our ideas emotionally. When you contemplate each of the options, listen to your mind and body. Take some time and get away from the crowd and people, then think about each option. You have already done your fact-finding; now tap into your body's reaction to each alternative. Every decision has its own pros and cons. You need to decide which option is the best fit for you and your needs. On a lighter note, lately, I have realized an easy way of making a choice. It might sound crazy to some. I toss a coin. Does that help arrive at a conclusion? In some sense, yes. We make our decision even before flipping the coin. Remember the last time you tossed a coin? Didn't you desire a specific outcome? Individuals frequently have a desired outcome that is impacted by their personal emotions, expectations, and beliefs.

   If you get the side that corresponds with what you want, you will cheerfully accept it and proceed with that choice; if not, you will feel dissatisfied. You can either be satisfied or disappointed with the outcome based on its alignment with your preferences.

Mistakes and challenges are inevitable, irrespective of your choice. Decisions are a stepping stone, not a rigid mold. When you decide, commit fully. Allow yourself to engage wholeheartedly, embracing the uncertainty and challenges.

While thinking of the option, look for the one that:
- Stands out from all other options.
- Provides a sense of thrill and excitement.
- Makes you feel relaxed.
- Aligns with who you are.

Choose what resonates most and trust yourself. Seek emotional alignment, a sense of excitement, and a feeling of relaxation. If an option closely mirrors your dream reality, it will naturally stand out. The issue is that we have stopped listening to our inner self and are often influenced by external world, which advocates the standard and known path.

"The grass is always greener on the other side," but beneath the allure lies the reality of unseen challenges. Trust your judgment, your gut, and the insights gained so far. Your choices shape your reality, and what you make of them molds your journey.

TRUST YOURSELF

"Life is about choices. Some we regret, some we're proud of. Some will haunt us forever. The message: we are what we chose to be." Graham Brown

N - NOW!

The runway is set; now it's time to take off. Converting knowledge into action is the key to achieving your aspirational life.

So far, you have taken actions to design the master plan of your desired life. Remember, things will change, plans can and will fail. But guess what? It's not the foolproof plan; it's the unwavering belief in yourself and that burning desire to turn those dreams into reality. If you are up for it, then do it now!

Postponing the start date might seem tempting, but it comes with potential consequences, including:

- Loss of momentum: You might lose the momentum and enthusiasm you initially had. This can make it more challenging to start and make progress on goals. The longer we delay, the harder it becomes to regain that momentum.
- Missed opportunities: Time-sensitive opportunities may pass, and we may find ourselves regretting the missed chances to achieve our goals or pursue our passions.
- Self-Confidence: Taking timely action helps build self-confidence, which is crucial for personal growth and success. When we consistently delay actions, our self-confidence can erode, and we may doubt our ability to achieve desired outcomes.
- Habit Formation: Taking action consistently is essential for forming positive habits. When we delay actions, we miss out on the opportunity to establish productive routines and reinforce desired behaviors.
- Overcoming Barriers: Taking immediate action allows us to address potential barriers or challenges sooner rather than later.

By taking action, we can identify and overcome obstacles more effectively, leading to better problem-solving skills and resilience.

- Positive Reinforcement: When we take action and make progress toward our goals, we experience a sense of accomplishment and satisfaction. This positive reinforcement motivates us to continue moving forward and maintain our momentum.

If you really want to succeed in your endeavor, embracing a bias for action is key. It's quite tempting to remain in a state of inaction.

Besides, I am not suggesting that you go in guns blazing and quit your current option. It will take time to get to your aspirational life. The time from now until reaching your aspirational life, utilize that time to carve out your path, gain skills, and experience the possibilities that resonate with your desired "To Be" reality. It's about gradual progression, taking steps that align with your goals. This journey to the life you envisioned won't happen overnight – it's a process. Remember, every step counts, and the journey itself is as valuable as the destination you're working towards.

When I was contemplating my option of flying, and I decided on Paragliding and getting trained for it, I was to get trained in Kamshet, and I had never been to that place. It takes roughly about a day to get there by train. My instructor, who is basically from Himachal, trains at a place called Bir, which is not very far from my city (just an overnight journey by bus). He had asked me to join him at Kamshet as he was there for a flying vacation. Above all, I would be the only student there. He generally teaches in Bir and in groups. This background was relevant because of the next part. To get to Kamshet, I had to travel via Pune, so I got an unconfirmed train ticket. That meant I would get a berth if there are cancellations corresponding to my position on the waitlist, or I would have to make do by sitting and sleeping on the floor. On the journey day, I was still unconfirmed, and that meant an uncertain and uncomfortable journey. Many of you might say, "what's the big deal." Well, not a big deal if that was the only choice I had. But I had a choice, stay back and maybe go next month to Bir and get trained there. That would have been a lot easier than this. Well, here I was faced with uncertainties about boarding with an unconfirmed ticket, I hesitated. I was still in two minds when the train started rolling out of the station. However, I seized the opportunity, and the resulting adventure was unforgettable. If you have ever experienced train journey in India, you'd understand the kind of adventures I'm referring to, especially when it is overbooked.

Similarly, while I was getting trained, I had just completed ground handling (practice handling the glider while on the ground) and had taken a few bunny hops (small flights from small hills). After that, I was happy with my progress until my instructor told me that I was to take a flight from Tower Hill. Some background: a bunny hop is a small flight from a small hill, a few meters above ground level, done in a calm and controlled environment. A flight from Tower Hill in Kamshet is not a small flight in comparison because of the height of the take-off point, which is close to around 250 meters, and after take-off, with the thermals, the sky is the limit. To a person who has been flying, this is an okay height, but not for me because I was graduating from hops to the real world, and that meant a lot, especially when it comes as a surprise to you.

Here I was on the last day of my training, sitting in a restaurant happily enjoying my plate of missal pav, thinking I am done with the training. That's when Gurpreet (my instructor) smiles at me and says, "Let's go and take a flight from Tower Hill." In a moment, from enjoying what I was eating, I was filled with fear. Fear of not just the height but also because I had seen a student pilot take off and dive into the hill that same morning. The pilot was uninjured and fine when she was rescued. So, I went up to the take-off area, which by itself is an adventure, praying that the weather turns and it gets canceled, but it didn't. Despite the fear and apprehensions, I took off. But the adventure did not end there. To add to it, after I took off, I lost my radio (it's the only way your instructor gives you instructions to steer and land). I had not instructions coming in and yet I landed safely. This was not only my first flight from a height of above 200 meters but also my first independent flight and landing, which usually happens after you have taken a dozen or more flights.

In moments of uncertainty, the mind often inclines towards comfort, making the path of discomfort all the more important.

It would have been very easy for me to just not board that train and go back home or not take that flight, yet I did. In fact, to be honest, I was inclined towards turning back both times, but I didn't. I have done that in the past; remember the incident in school where I ran away from reciting a story? But I am happy that I didn't let that part of my mind, which was not in favor of taking this journey, take over. Changing our lives often encounters resistance from ingrained thinking patterns and habits. Overthinking can lead to confusion, often prompting us to choose the simplest way out. It's not that I haven't backed out after that; I did, but lately, it's been more accepting and going ahead with the task than backing out.

A fascinating read, 'The 5 Second Rule' by Mel Robbins, offers an effective technique. Count backward from 5 to 1 and take action. You take one step (action), however small it may be, it gets you closer to your goal by that one step. Overthinking grants time for excuses to flourish, holding you within your comfort zone.

Our brains instinctively protect us from discomfort, opting for the easiest solutions – which often involve avoiding action. These patterns are cultivated over time, born from years of experience.

Waiting for Motivation

Don't. It's not going to come. The best option is to inspire yourself and take action. While you may seek inspiration from external sources like talking to people or reading books, true inspiration comes from within. You need to have a clear goal and take consistent actions to keep pushing yourself, creating enough momentum to achieve what you wish for.

Just like a car won't move without being put in gear, your aspirations require your active engagement. Waiting for motivation to strike won't help; the real magic happens when you initiate action.

"An idea, no matter how good it is, is useless unless acted upon." *Thomas Edison*

It's not easy to quit and start something new, but you don't have to. Instead, you can:

- Begin with small steps to build momentum gradually.
- Develop strategies to overcome limitations that hinder your progress.
- Structure your days with tasks, celebrating each achievement. Grab a beer or a coffee, have an ice cream, or whatever you like.
- Prioritize tasks, as not everything is equally important, and multitasking isn't effective. Focus on one task at a time.
- Ask for help from friends, colleagues, family, or maybe a coach who can guide you.
- Hold yourself accountable for what you have started.
- Make sure to set aside time between days to take breaks and rejuvenate.

Your Blueprint

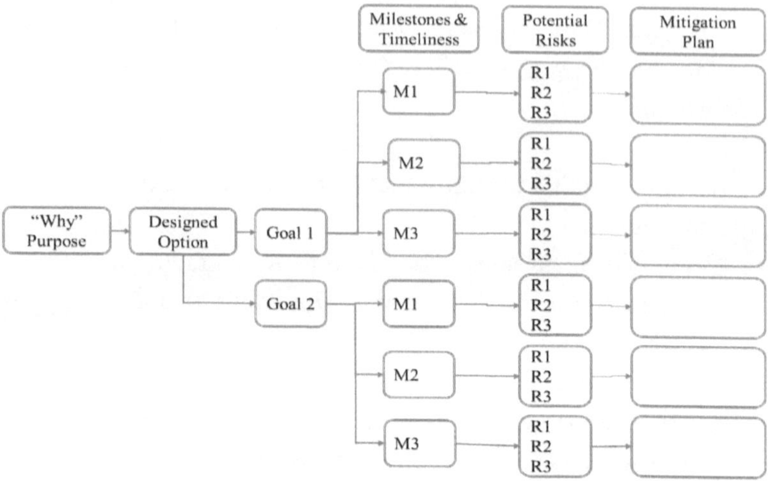

Note: You will have multiple goals to achieve your desired reality

Milestones:

Setting a goal, whether it's personal or professional, is important. However, achieving that goal can become overwhelming without a plan. Many times, we hesitate to take action because we get stuck in our thoughts, such as "where to start" or "what if."

That's why defining milestones before diving into action is crucial. Milestones play a pivotal role in helping individuals stay on track and make progress toward their goals. These milestones are small, manageable steps that lead to the desired outcome. They act as a guide, ensuring one stays on course and provide a sense of accomplishment as you work toward reaching your goal.

Consider the goal of writing a book. If the goal is simply to write a book, it can feel daunting and discouraging, and you may never take action. Thoughts like "it will take too much time," "where do I source the information," "how would I get it published," "will it sell," and many more may occupy your mind, leading to inaction due to a lack of answers. The enormity of the task can result in feeling overwhelmed, stuck in overthinking mode, anxious, and struggling to maintain focus and motivation. As I am writing this, I am having all these thoughts.

Breaking down the goals into several achievable steps and following them through one at a time increases the chances of success. Steps like:

- Research on the topic
- Creating an outline
- Writing chapters according to the outline
- First draft
- Copyediting and revision
- Finalize
- Submit to the publisher
- Note – You can break these milestones into sub-milestones as well.

The benefit of defining these small, manageable steps is that you can measure your progress. It also provides the flexibility to assess and improvise your strategy if you see yourself drifting from the path that you have decided.

Breaking down your journey into structured, manageable chunks is much better than pursuing a long-term goal like writing a book with unforeseen challenges or obstacles. By pursuing smaller, attainable milestones while keeping the larger goal in the back of your mind, you can maintain clarity and concentration, reducing the chances of feeling overwhelmed or discouraged.

Organizing your journey into these manageable chunks will lighten your cognitive load and provide motivation as you achieve one step after another, offering a sense of accomplishment with each milestone reached.

It's important to realize that, just like traveling a long distance, you don't cover the whole distance in one go. You plan your trip, make iterations, and take detours as needed to reach your destination.

Similarly, in our life's journey, we need to create those milestones and be open to iterating along the way. If it were a simple, straight path, it would undoubtedly be easier, but life is often filled with twists and turns.

Creating Effective Milestones

- Start by writing the specific goal at the top of a piece of paper. It can be a personal, professional, or academic goal.
- Identify all possible tasks that you believe are necessary to achieve that goal. Brainstorm and consider what resources would be required.
- Prioritize those tasks based on logic and importance.
- Refine the list if necessary, ensuring it is well-organized and logically structured.
- Mention all the potential challenges and constraints associated with each step, and ways to mitigate those challenges. While you may not anticipate all challenges upfront, try to be proactive in identifying as many as possible.
- Along with these challenges and constraints, create a mitigation plan for each one.
- Set realistic timelines for each task, considering potential challenges. Ensure that your timeline is not overly ambitious and seems achievable.
- Create a visual roadmap or chart that illustrates the sequence of tasks and milestones.
- Hold yourself accountable for your progress. Share your plan with a friend or find an accountability partner who can help keep you on track.

Lastly, but not least, set up a reward system for achieving milestones or completing tasks. Celebrating your successes reinforces positive behavior and encourages continued effort.

S - CELEBRATE SUCCESS

Success requires commitment and action, but it's not solely about that. You should celebrate each achievement along the way to maintain your momentum.

"We are all capable of much more than we think we can."

When you begin to realize this and challenge the status quo to clear each milestone, you start reprogramming your belief system. As you continue forward, it reinforces your belief in your abilities to overcome any challenge.

You begin to form new habits, develop new skills, build character, and gain self-awareness.

Imagine all the challenges you have overcome while designing your life and celebrate each one.

BONUS - GET MORE

In today's time, where everyone is busy, how do you take time out for this?

So, you've got big dreams, right? The kind that could transform your life? Fantastic! But wait, have you considered your plan to deal with distractions that are experts at luring you away from this journey? In the old days, distractions might have included sports like street cricket, football, television shows, or meeting friends. Nowadays, that small handheld piece of tech has taken over.

Imagine yourself on the brink of your transformative journey, but before you take that life-changing step, think about the temptation to indulge in innocent videos of adorable furballs on Instagram or Facebook, not to mention the allure of memes and the endless scroll.

Have you fallen into the "I'll start tomorrow" trap? You know, the one where you say, "I'm going to start exercising tomorrow, after I watch videos on how to do it, after I buy myself good sneakers, after I get running clothes, after I find some motivation, after the temperature becomes a bit more pleasant." I'm sure we've all been guilty of this in one way or another.

I understand that it might seem like a demanding request, but it's a necessary one if you're truly committed to achieving your goals. To gain more, you'll have to do less of certain things before embarking on this journey. Less mindless scrolling through social media, fewer elaborate excuses you've been concocting, and fewer activities that are preventing you from starting your transformational journey now!

Because honestly, if you don't start now, when will you? When the time is right? When everything is perfectly okay? Probably not. The time is now!

Here's how:

The first thing you need to do is analyze your day. How are you spending your day going about your tasks?

I had a personal revelation when I analyzed my own actions. I was preparing for an upcoming management review, and my task was to create a draft PowerPoint presentation for that review. I had a couple of hours set aside to complete this task, and I knew exactly what I needed to present, so it should have taken me a maximum of an hour to put it all together. Easy peasy, right?

Well, I did manage to prepare the draft and sent it to my bosses for review. However, when I later reviewed what I had accomplished during the day, I realized that I could have been much more productive. Essentially, I had only utilized around 40% of my time on actual productive tasks. The rest of my time was devoted to activities that had no bearing on my main goal.

Furthermore, I noticed that this wasn't just a one-off occurrence; it happened almost daily. Some might argue that it's about working smartly, but I realized that I could have achieved more in my day if I hadn't spent time on unproductive activities.

Imagine if you could reclaim some of those hours during the day to work on your life goals? Then you can't say "I don't have time."

1. Declutter – Identify and eliminate anything that doesn't serve your goals. Identify the distractions in your life that hinder your daily progress. These may include:

- Social media and other addictive forms of technology that consume excessive time and attention.
- Interruptions and distractions from others, such as phone calls, emails, and messages.
- Procrastination, the habit of postponing important tasks.

- Lack of motivation or enthusiasm for the task at hand.
- Overthinking, self-doubt, and self-criticism.
- Poor time management and planning.
- Personal habits and lifestyle choices that divert your focus.
- Environmental distractions like noise and clutter.

To eliminate these distractions, you must first be aware of what's holding you back.

2. Organize – Put things in order. Recognize the triggers for these distractions and categorize them into:

- Time – Getting engrossed in critical tasks while already occupied with something else.
- Environment – Inappropriate locations and distracting surroundings.
- People – Unsupportive individuals, social pressures, comparisons.
- Systems – Technology addiction, particularly related to social media.
- Beliefs – Fear of success, fear of failure, self-doubt.
  Situations/Circumstances – Past failures and setbacks.

3. Implement and Inspect – Not everything is important, so you need to prioritize and set your boundaries to minimize disruptions and stay focused on the task. It's not as easy as it sounds, so it's a continuous process requiring consistent effort and evaluation.

Mark my words, you will fail, but through mindfulness, self-awareness, and developing good habits, you can address them as they arise.

Having an accountability partner can be helpful to provide the level of accountability and support required to keep you on track. This helps in:

- Keeping you accountable for the goals you have set for yourself
- Keeping you motivated, focused, and driven
- Overcoming obstacles

- Identifying disruptors
- Serving as a sounding board for your thoughts and providing feedback
- Building good habits
- Finding someone whom you can trust and are comfortable sharing your dreams and goals

Technology can also help minimize distractions. Example like "focus" mode on phone, time management apps, phone settings that restrict usage of apps etc.

4. Control – Manage through increased self-awareness of your own thoughts, feelings, and behaviors to better understand the triggers and patterns. Practice focusing on the task at hand.

- Set smaller and achievable goals for yourself as you achieve them; this will build confidence and motivate you to keep going.
- Develop a routine and a schedule.
- Practice time management by prioritizing tasks. Use the Eisenhower Matrix.

"I have two problems, the urgent and that important. The urgent are not important and the important are not urgent" Dwight D. Eisenhower

Importance			
	Important	**Do it NOW!**	**Plan it**: can do later
	Not Important	**Delegate it**: you don't need to do it yourself	**Chuck it!**
		Urgent	**Not urgent**
	Urgency		

Eisenhower Matrix

5. Habit – Is it a habit yet? Repeat until it becomes second nature. We talked about the activities during the day, but what about the thoughts that keep coming into our minds during the day, impacting our outcomes? By identifying those empowering and disempowering thoughts during the day, we improve our chances of addressing them rather than remaining oblivious to their impact.

Identify the event triggers and the thoughts associated with those events and what they resulted in, either a positive action for your growth or inaction.

As you go about recording for a few days, you will identify certain thought patterns and triggers for those thoughts emerging that will either be "empowering" and serving you or "disempowering" and not serving you.

Empowering thoughts need to stay; the disempowering ones definitely need to go.

You will get more out of your day by claiming more of your mind. To progress, you need to free up your mind from thoughts that are not serving you well.

Get more out of your day

Declutter

What needs to go?	Distractions (WhatApp, Calls unless urgent) Multi-tasking
Why	Hampering focus toward the task at hand

Organize

Disrupter *(time, place, people, systems)*	Time- picking up the task at the peak production time Place- doing work where there is lot of distraction Systems- Easy access to phone, mails Prioritization- Tasks not prioritized
Goal	Reduce time on phone, use it when free Avoid multitasking, assign task priority, non-urgent tasks can wait

Implement & Inspect

Plan	Prioritize tasks Find a location with least distraction for critical tasks Put phone on DND for an hour and switch off emails for an hour
Actual (post implementation)	Working as per priority list Doing critical tasks in meeting rooms

GAP

Control

Manage	Self-awareness and deliberate practice

Habit

Is it a Habit yet?	Getting there

One at a time

Finally, as we approach the conclusion of 'Transformation through ACTIONS!' and prepare to embark on the journey of living a purpose-driven life, remember that you have the power to transform your life through ACTIONS! So, go forth with determination, embrace the challenge of change, and claim the life you've always imagined.

Best of luck on your journey.

TO MY DEAR READERS

Thank you for embarking on this journey with me, a journey initiated by the simple act of purchasing this book.

Your decision to explore 'Transformation Through ACTIONS!' shows your commitment to your personal growth and transformation. I appreciate your trust in me and the ACTIONS framework. I hope the insights and wisdom shared in the book have inspired you to take action towards your transformation and realize your true potential.

Remember, the journey toward personal growth and transformation is an ongoing process, and I am here to support you on this journey. If you'd like to explore personal coaching, want to have a conversation about your dreams and aspirations, or have any questions related to the ACTIONS framework, please don't hesitate to reach out.

You can connect with me through my website www. abhishekbudhraja.com. There, you'll find valuable resources and information. You can also email me at contact@abhishekbudhraja. com. Additionally, you can also find me on social media platforms such as Facebook and LinkedIn. Feel free to send me a message or connect with me, and I'll be delighted to assist you on your journey of personal growth and your quest for a more meaningful and purpose-driven life.

Your success and transformation matter to me, and I'm excited to be part of your journey.

With gratitude and best wishes
Abhishek Budhraja

www.ingramcontent.com/pod-product-compliance
Lightning Source LLC
Chambersburg PA
CBHW021439150726

47989CB00001B/303